Beautiful Flowers
Grayscale Coloring Book

46 Stress Relieving Flowers with Positive Words

Copyright 2018
All Rights Reserved
Stephanie Alterman

Other coloring books on Amazon by Stephanie Alterman

Adult Grayscale Swear Words Coloring Book: A weapon against stress and anxiety. 41 designs of animals, flowers, icebergs and landscapes.

Beautiful Birds: Grayscale Coloring Book: 38 birds with inspirational and motivational Bible verses.

Inspirational Grayscale Coloring Book.

Hello everyone.

Thank you very much for purchasing this coloring book. My hope is for you to enjoy coloring the different patterns in the book.

Please leave a review

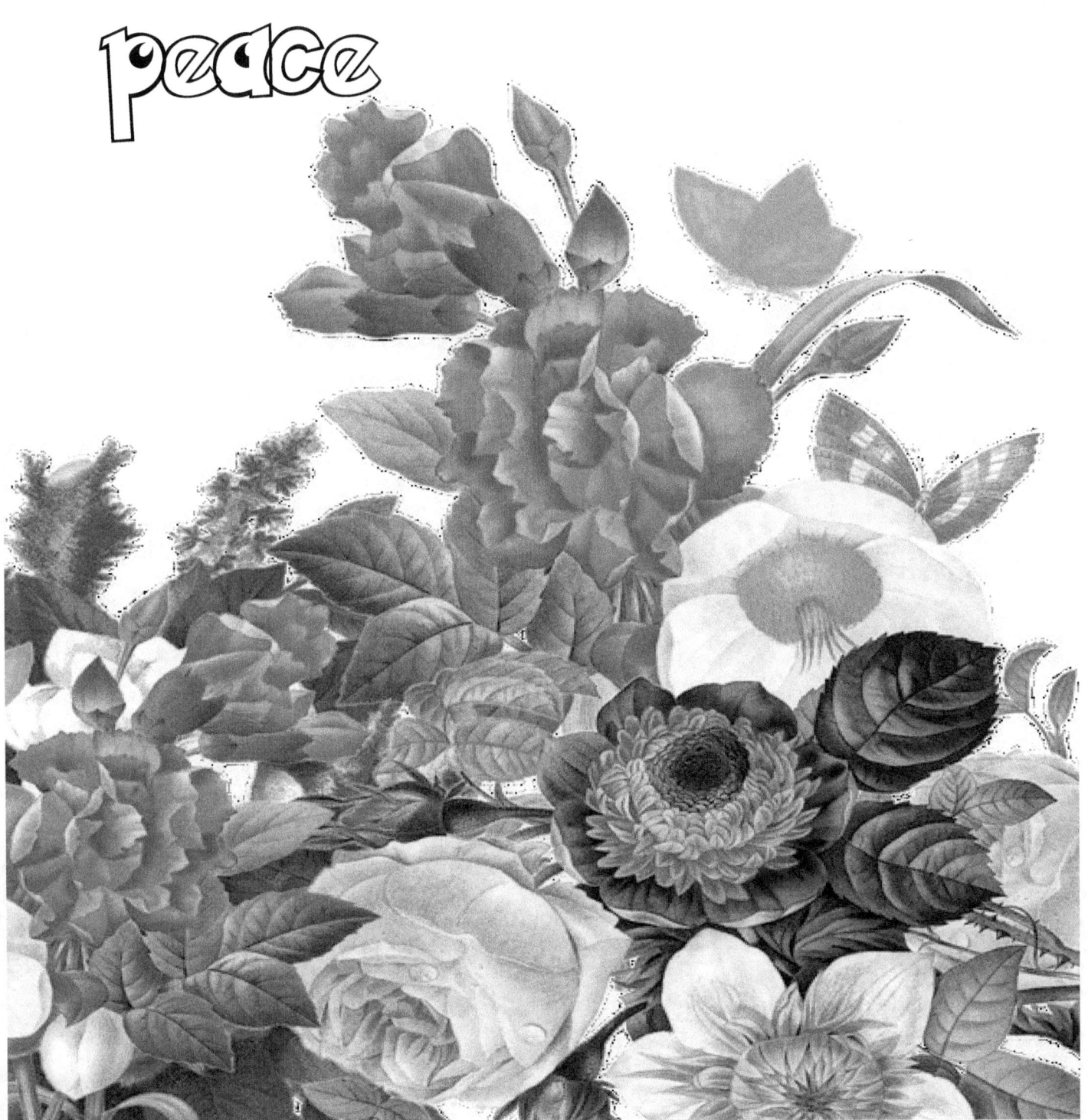

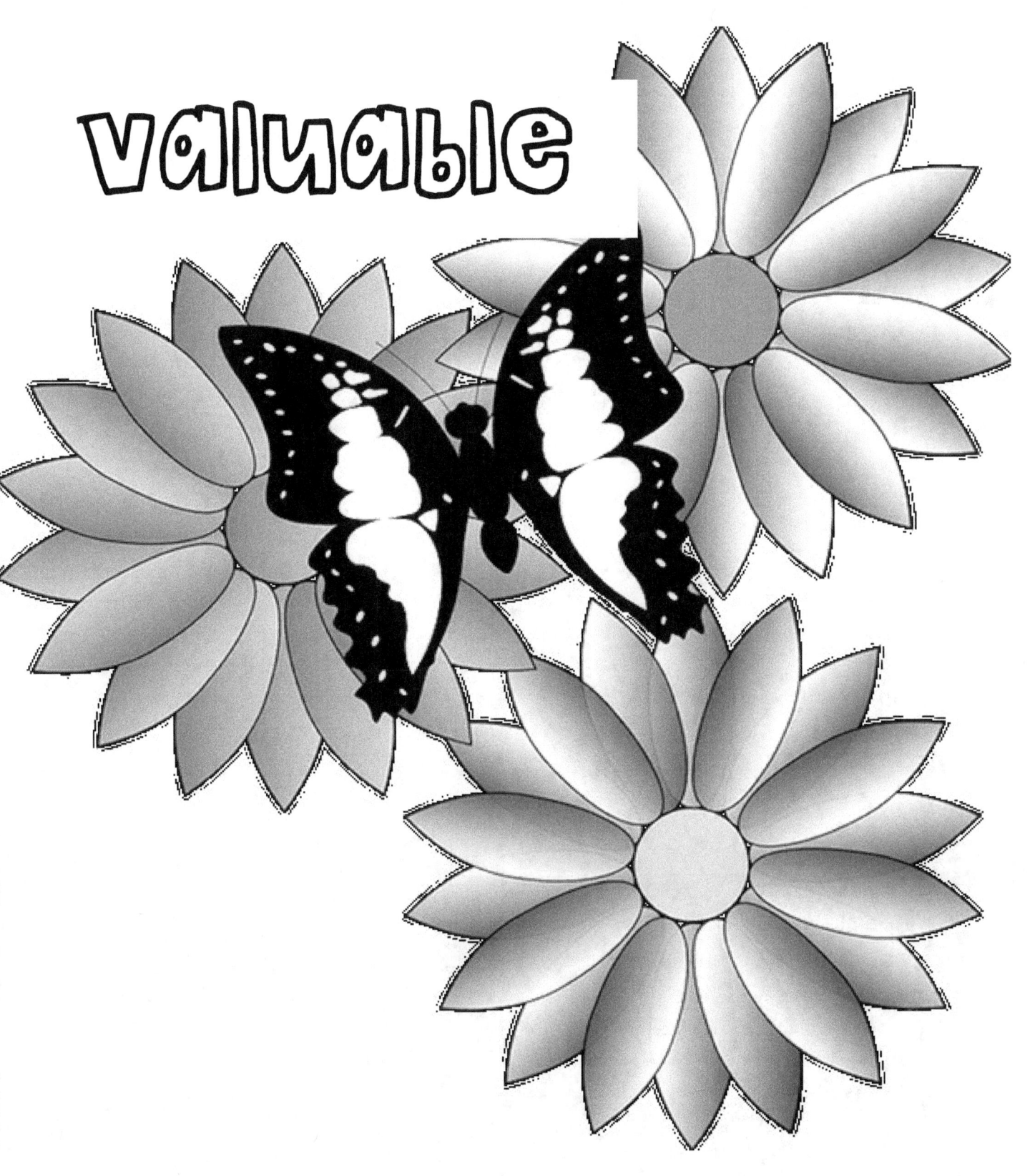

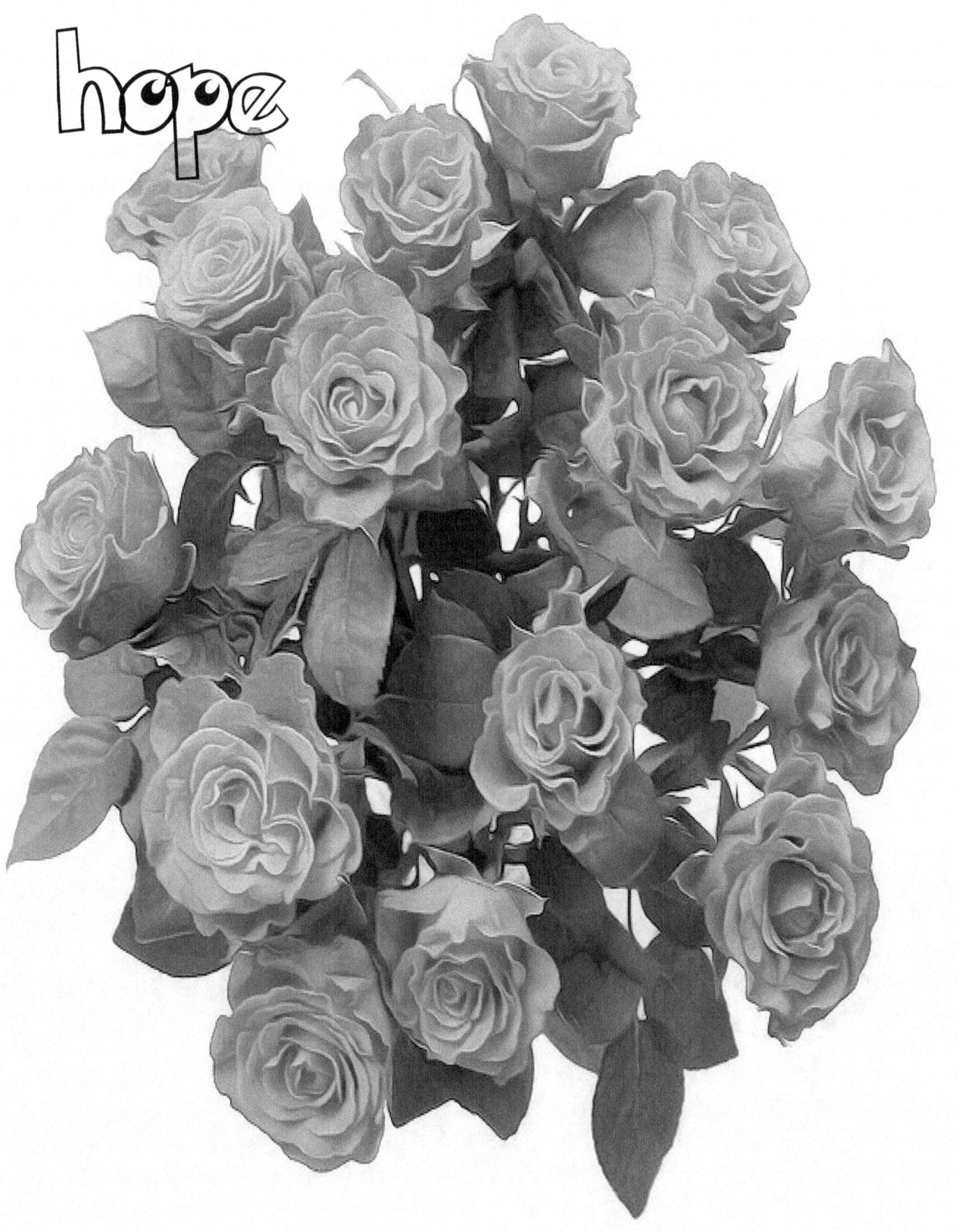

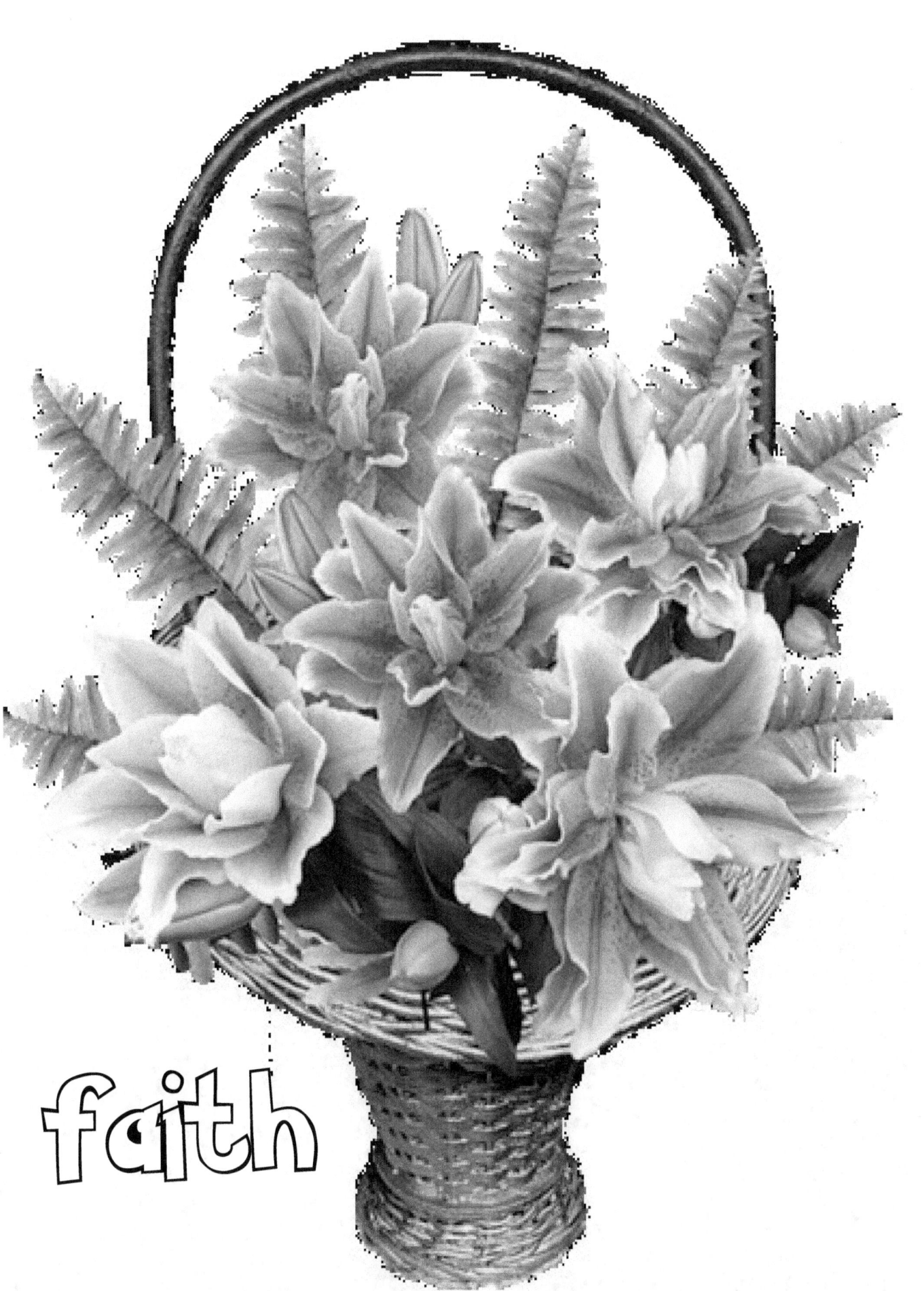

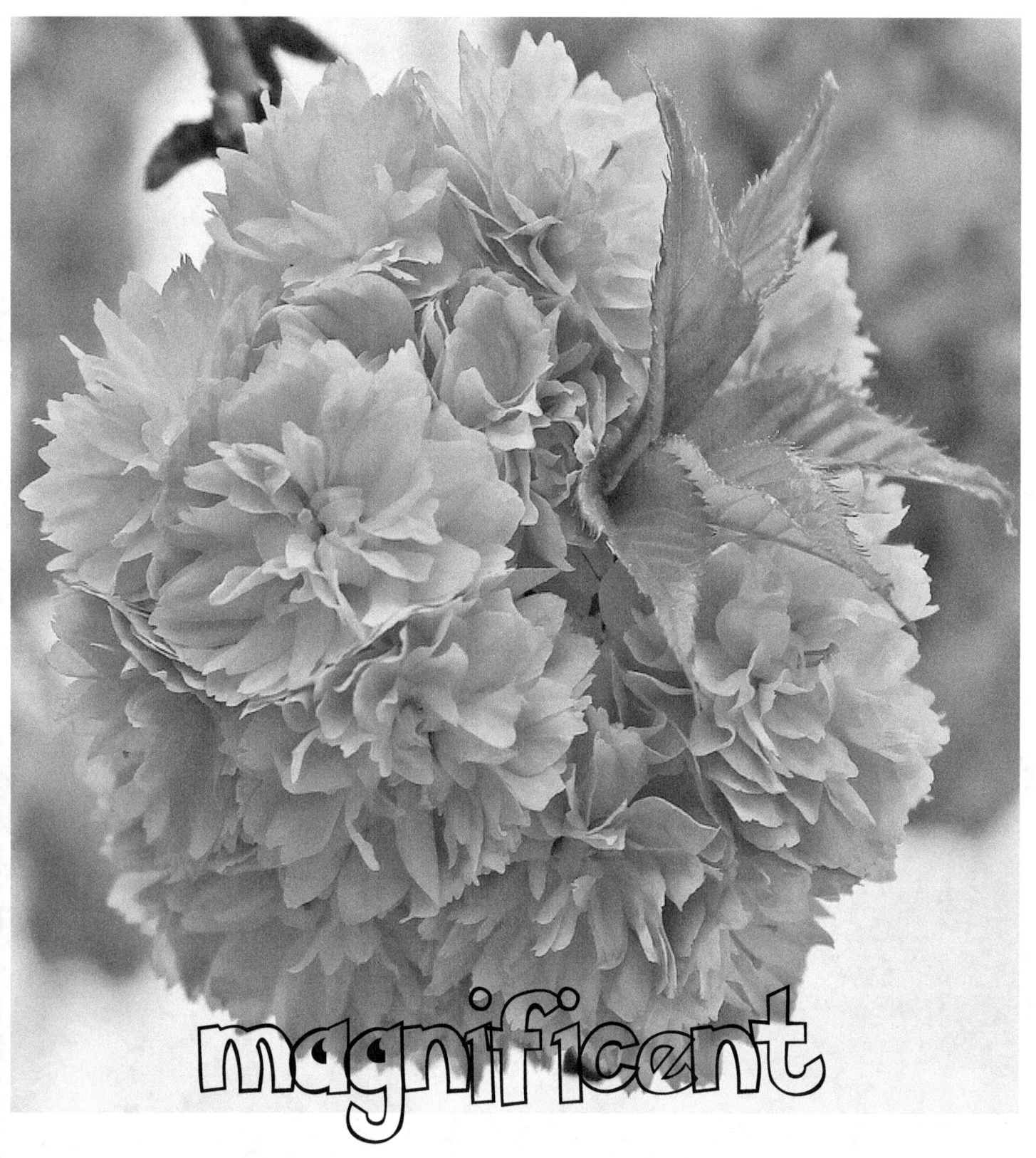

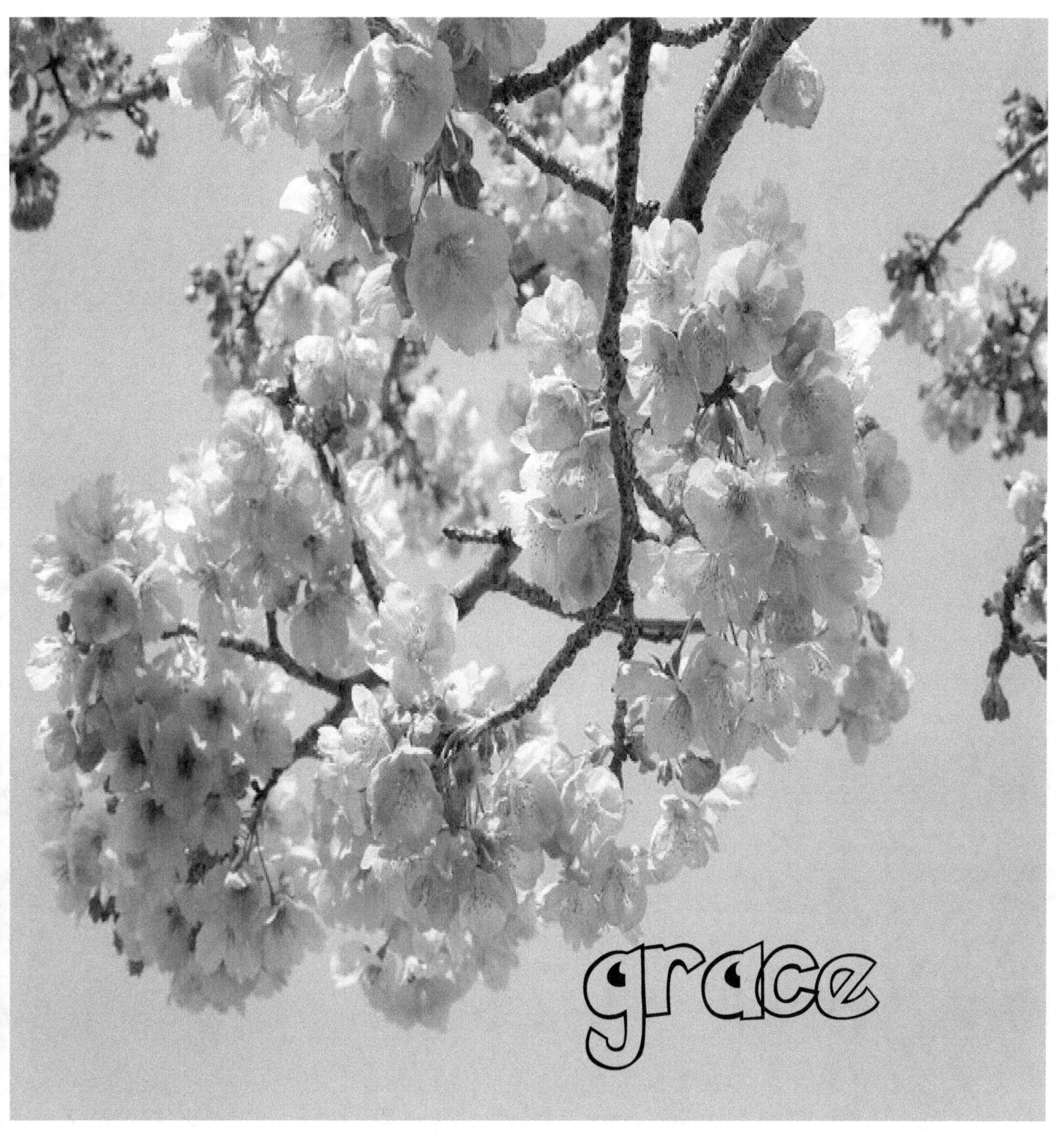

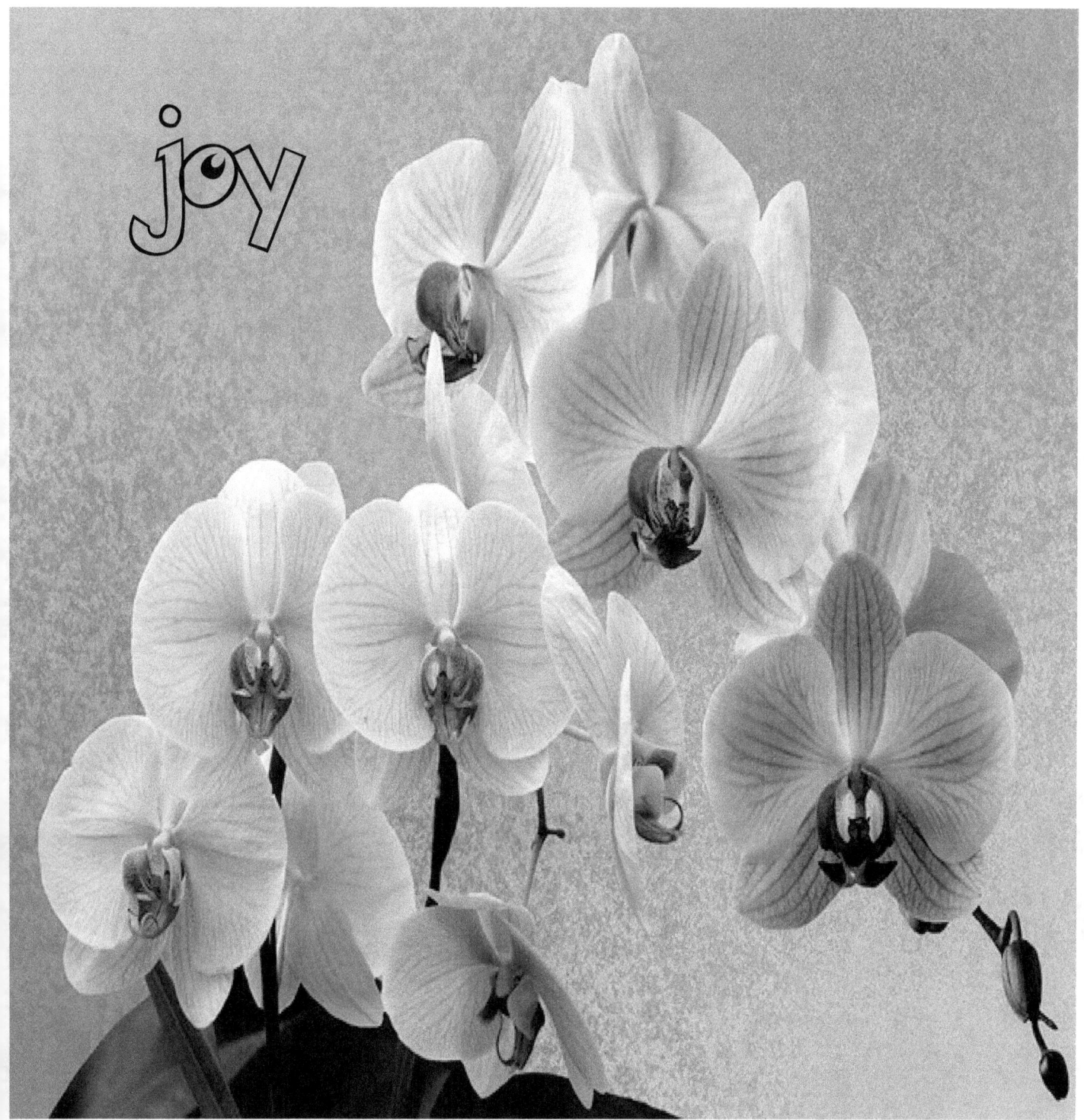

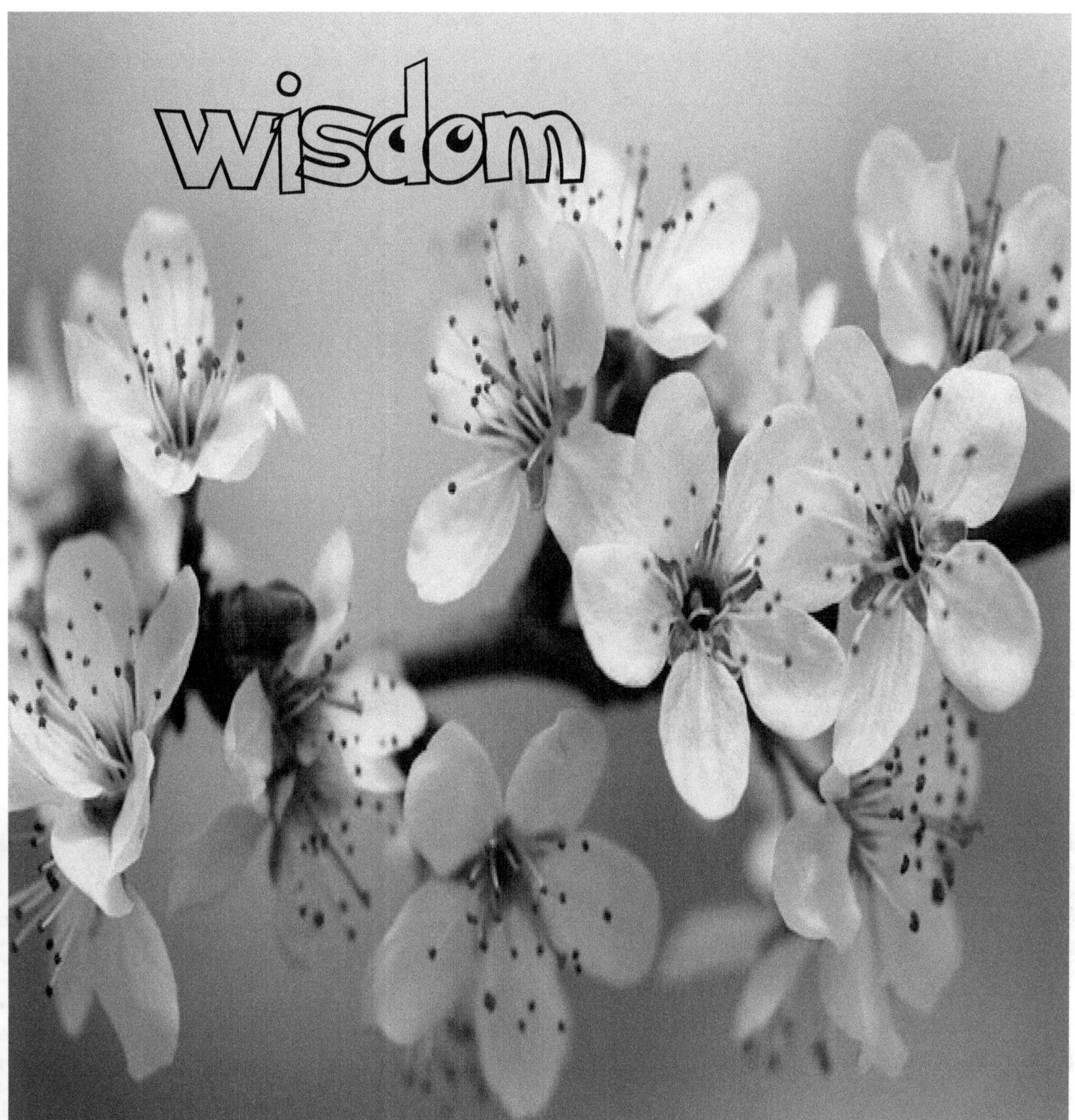

blessed

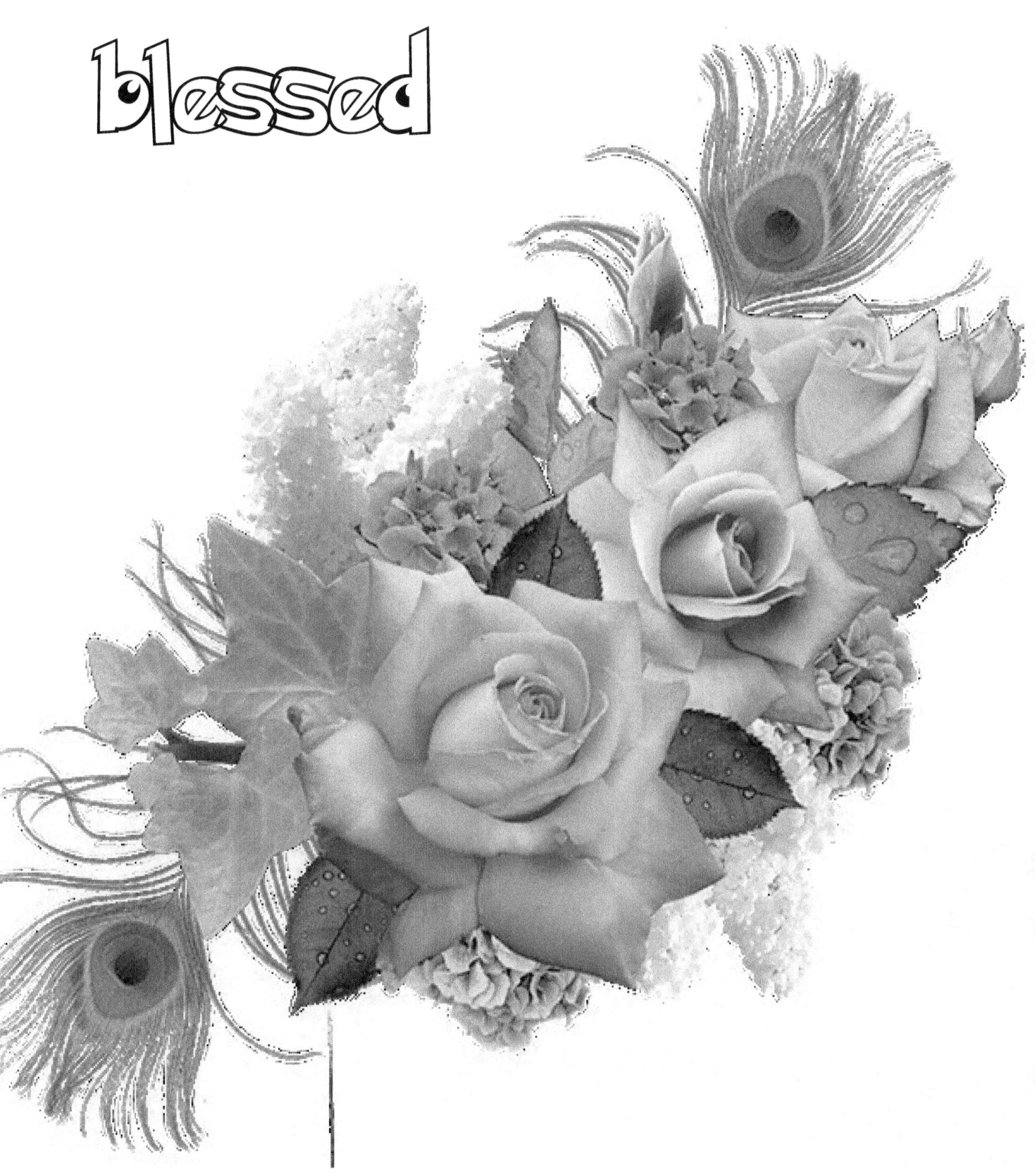

kindness

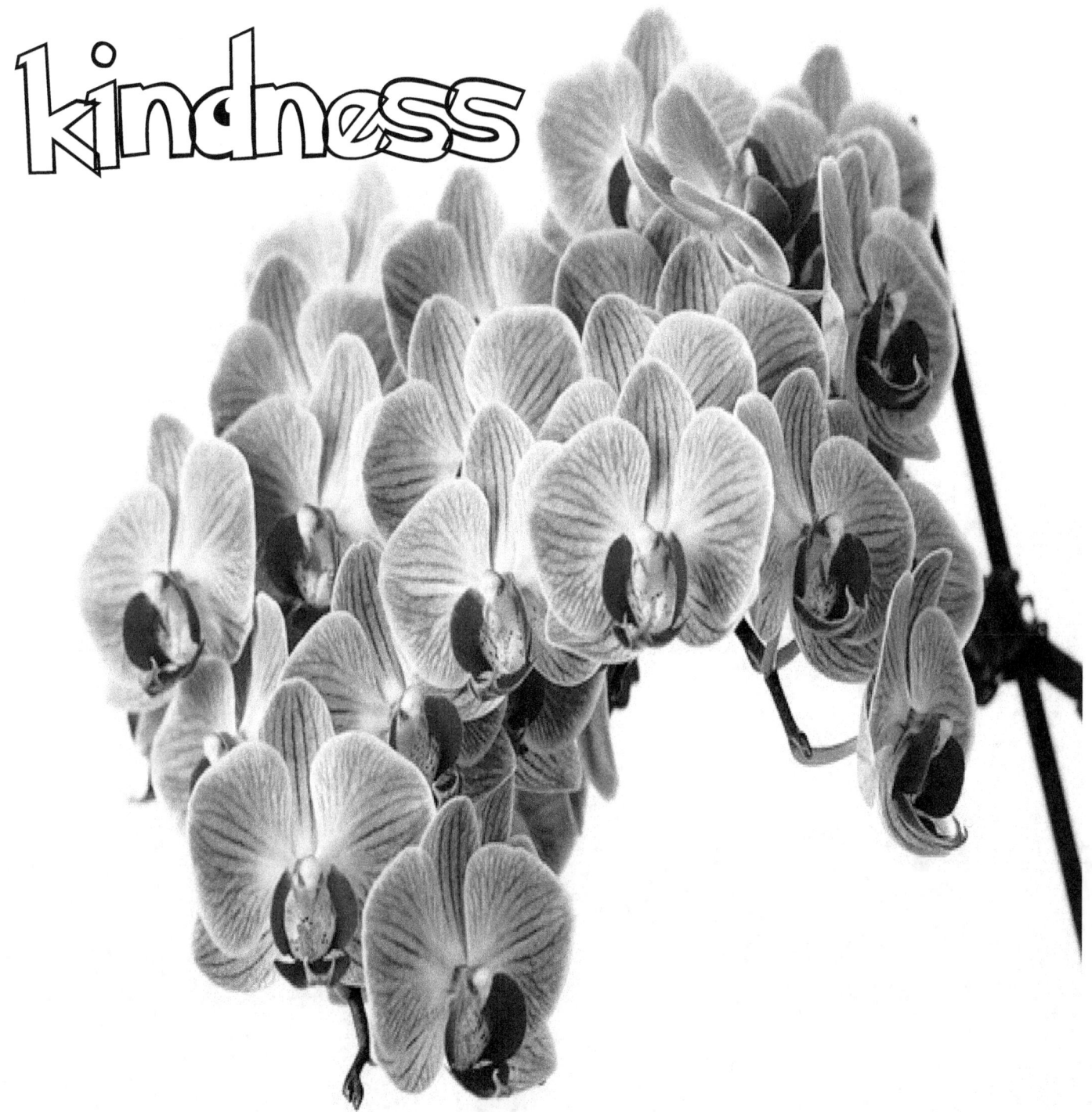

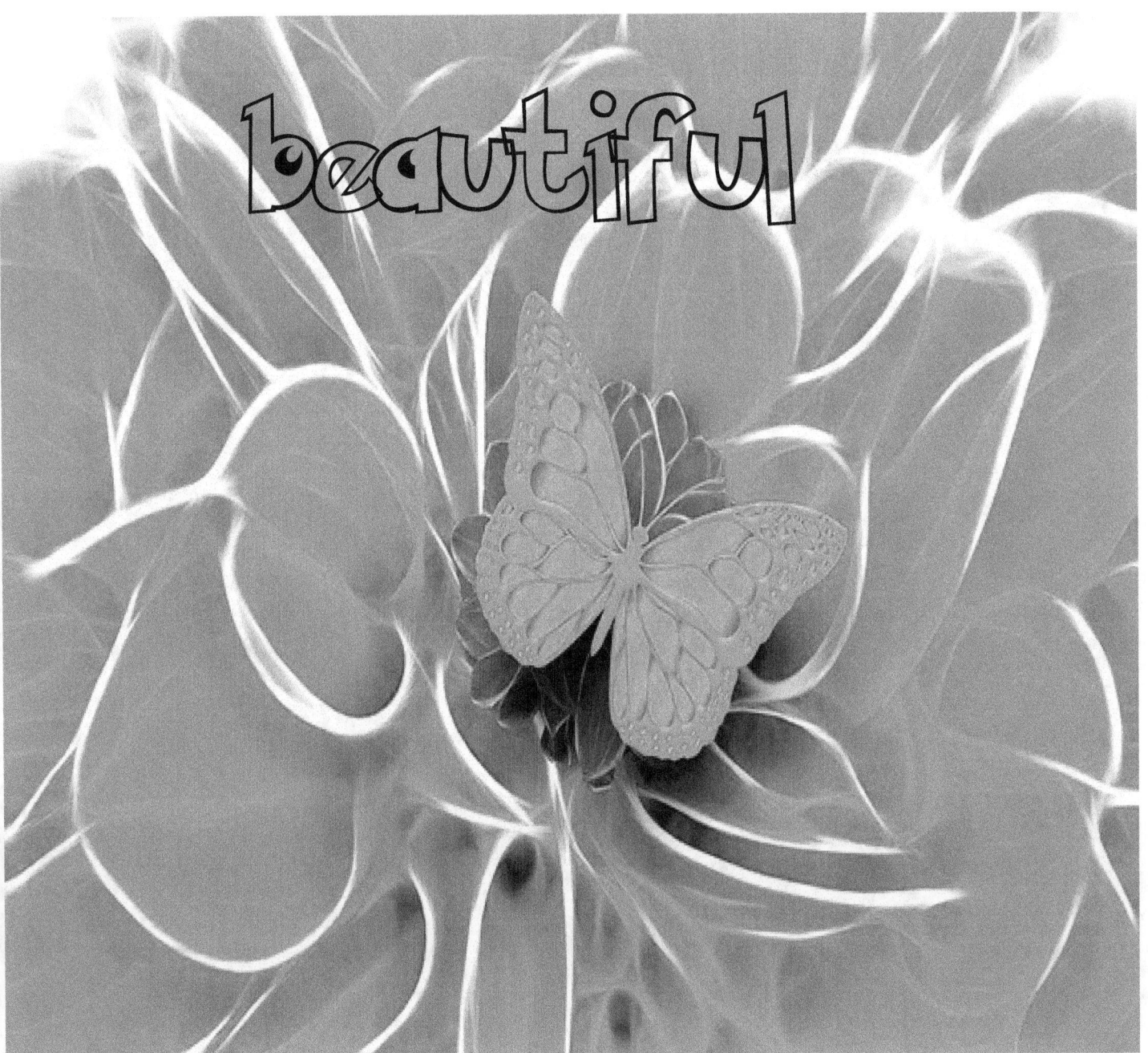

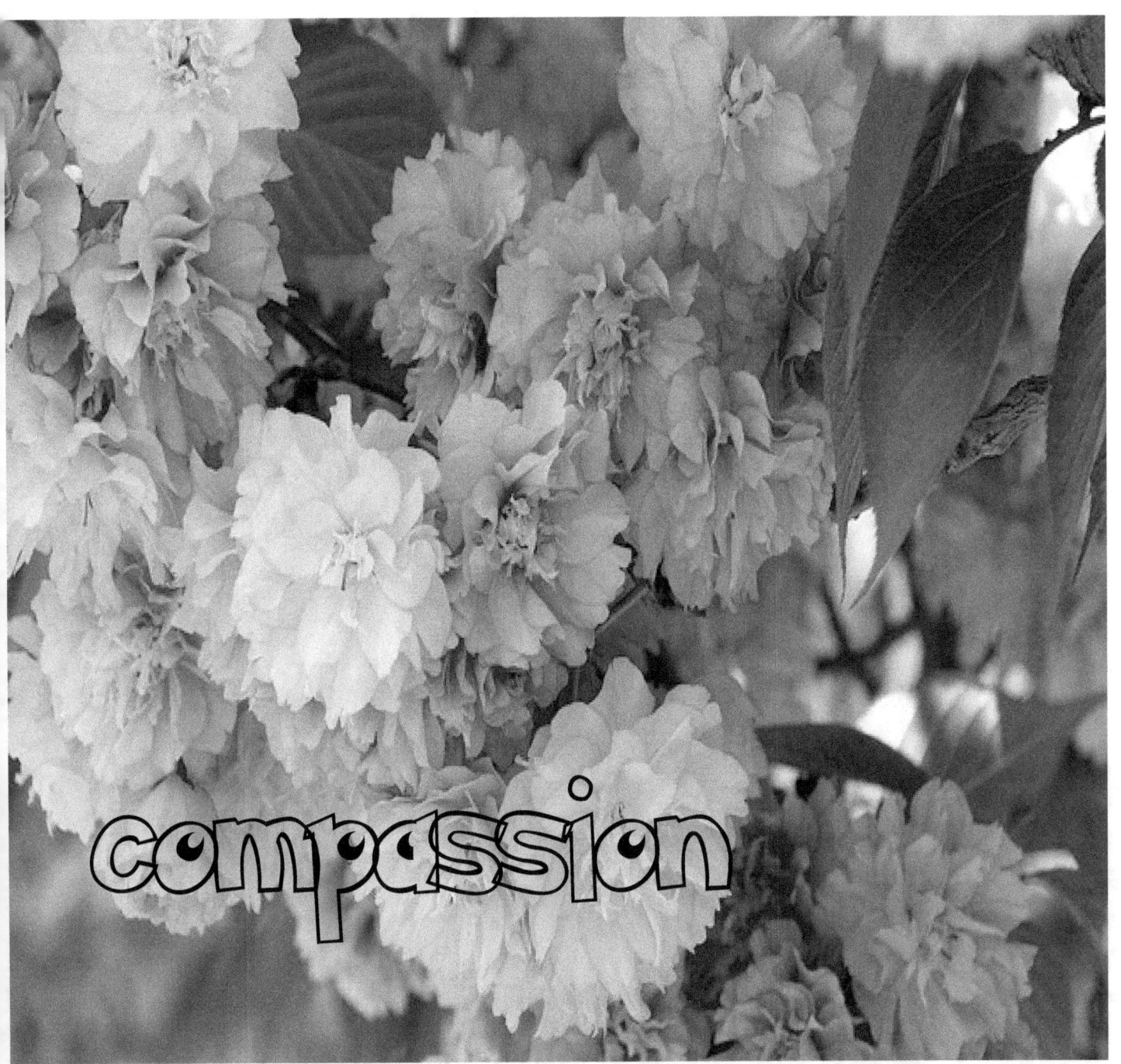

empowered

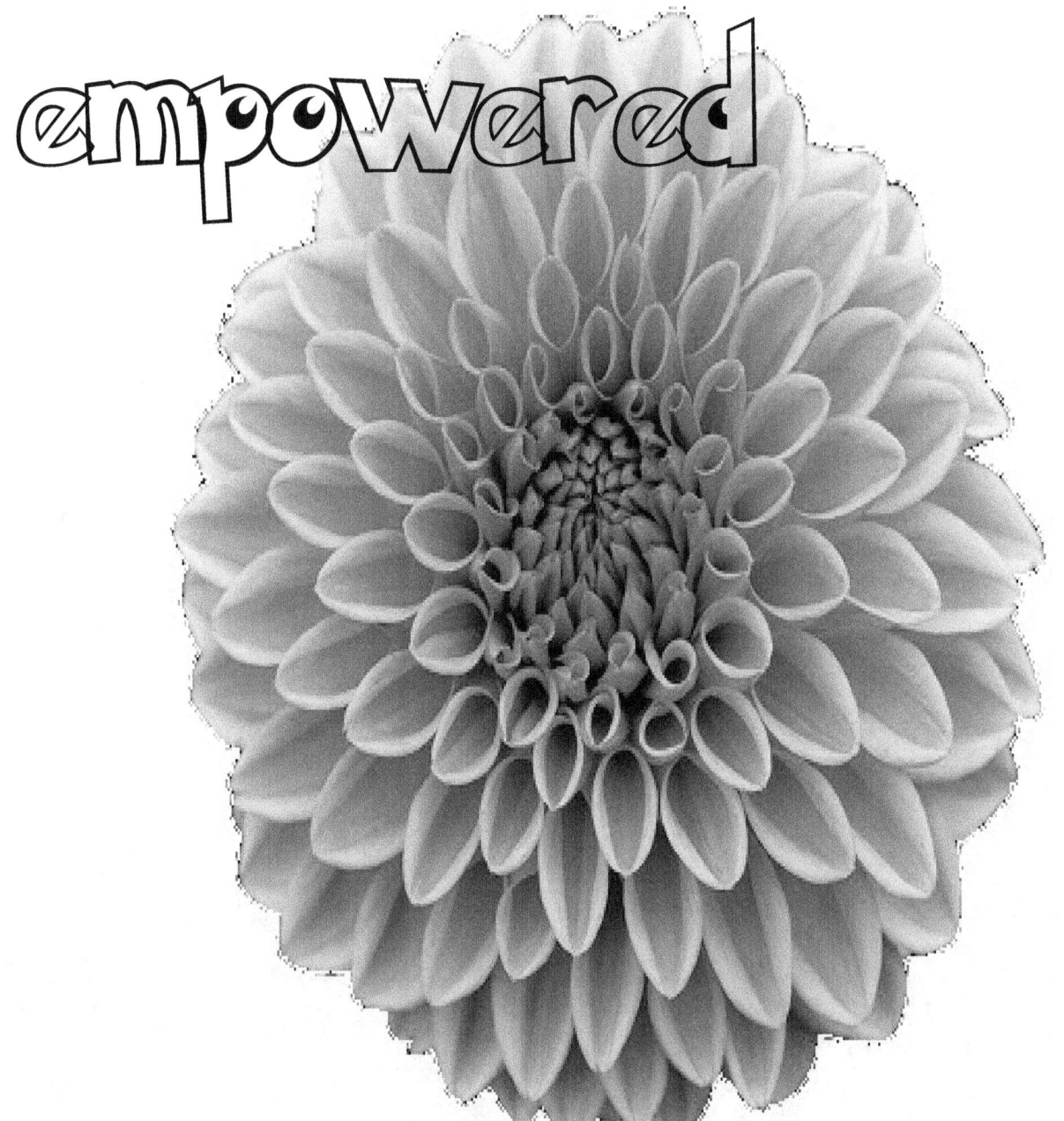

calm

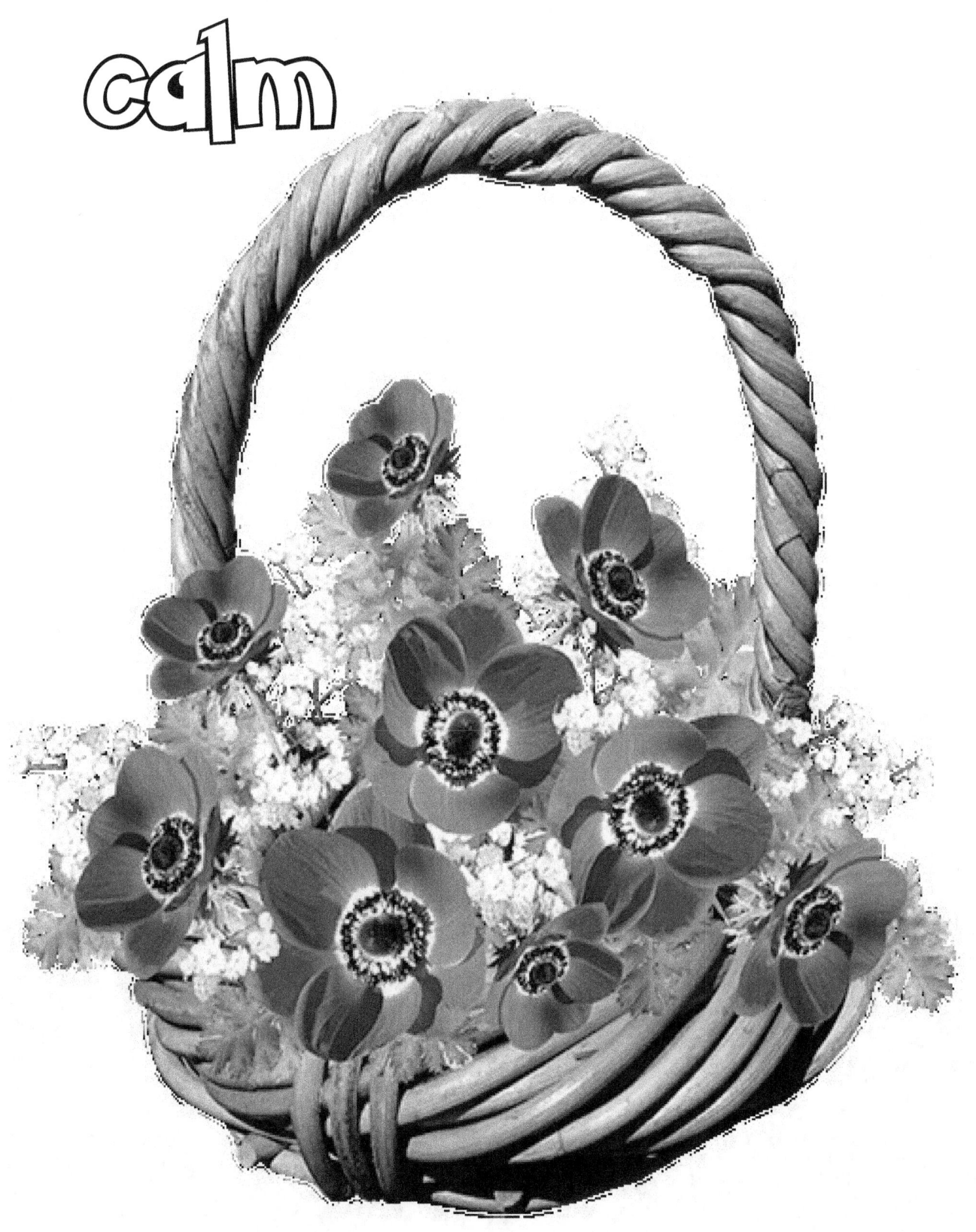

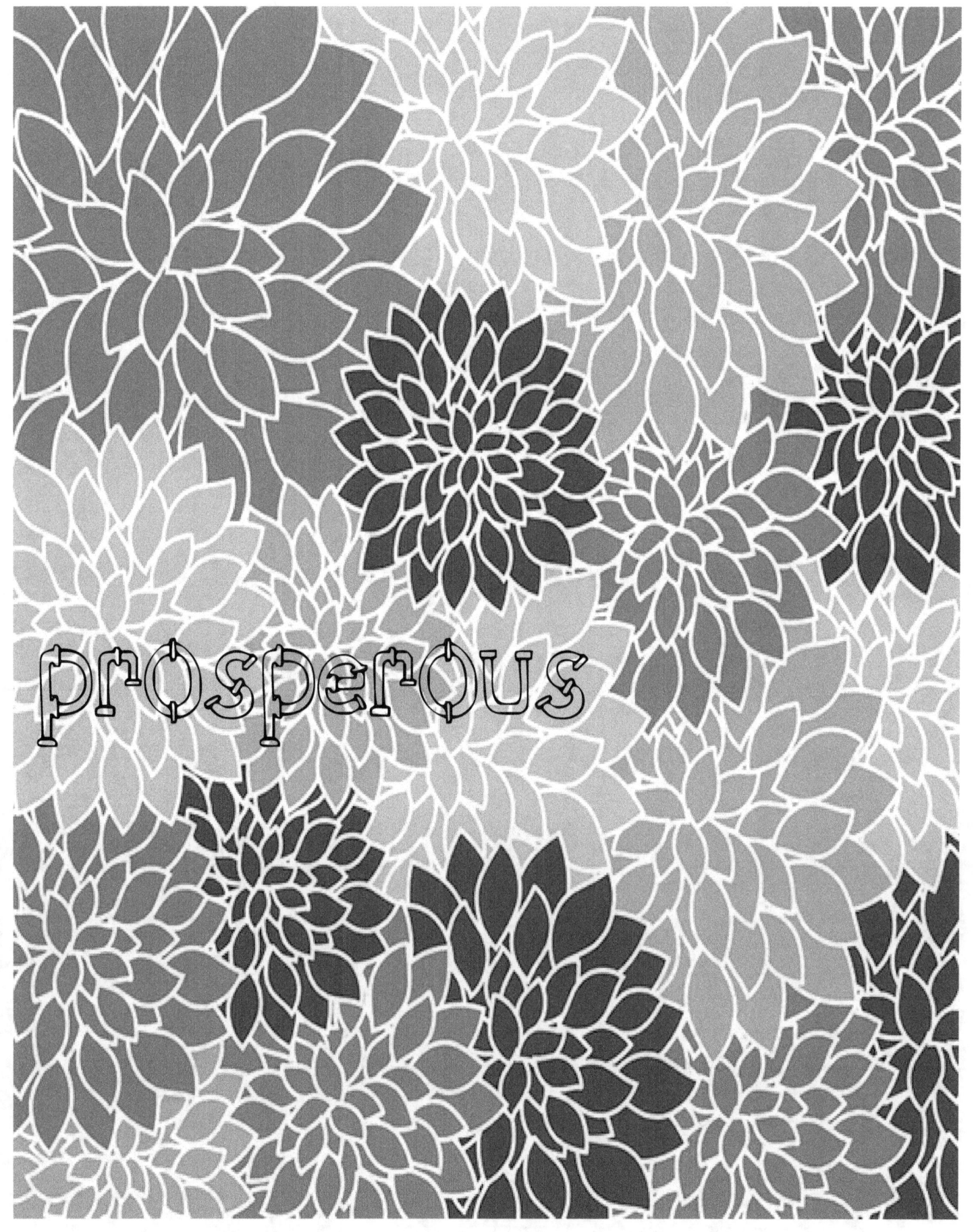

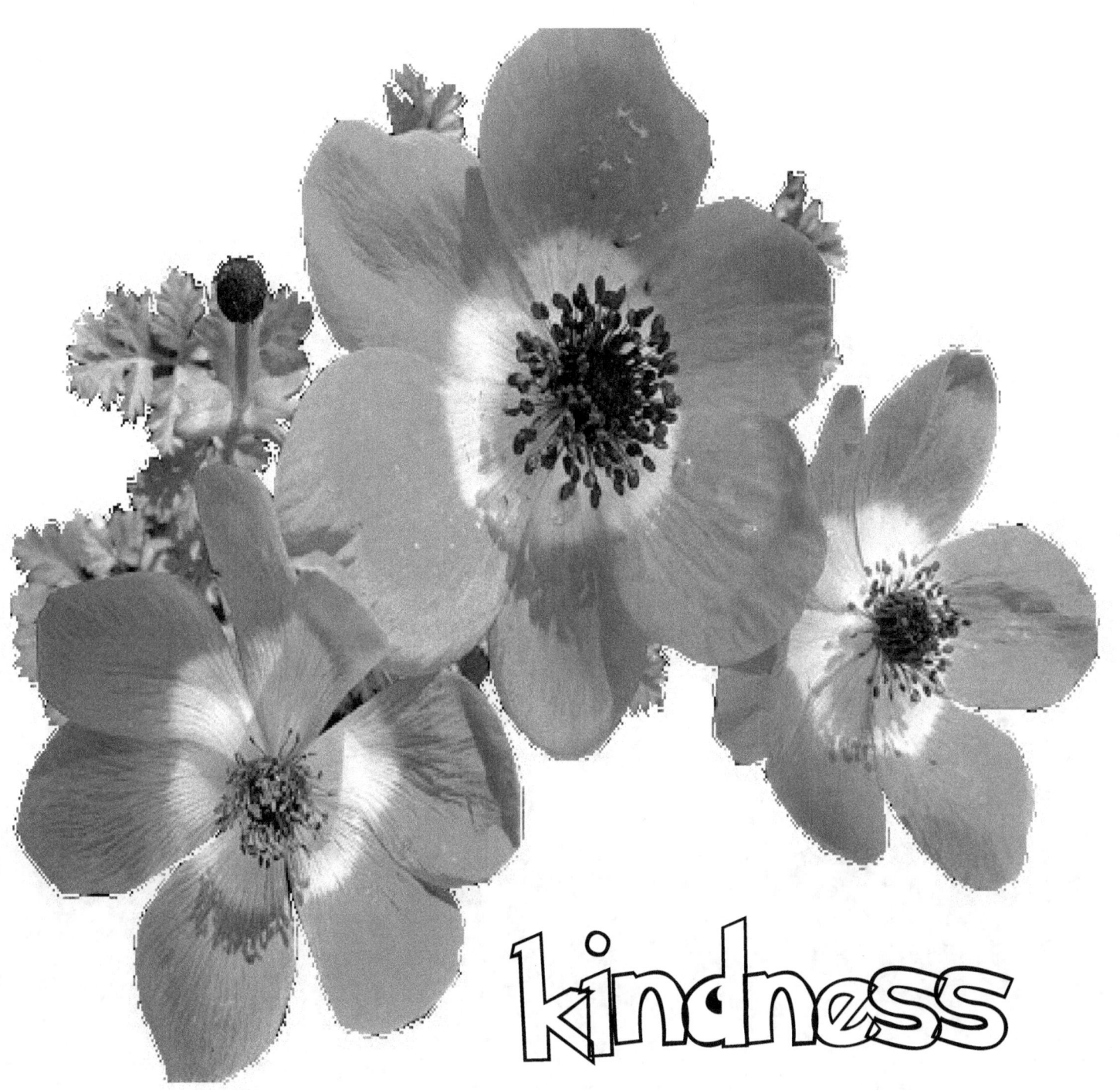

believe

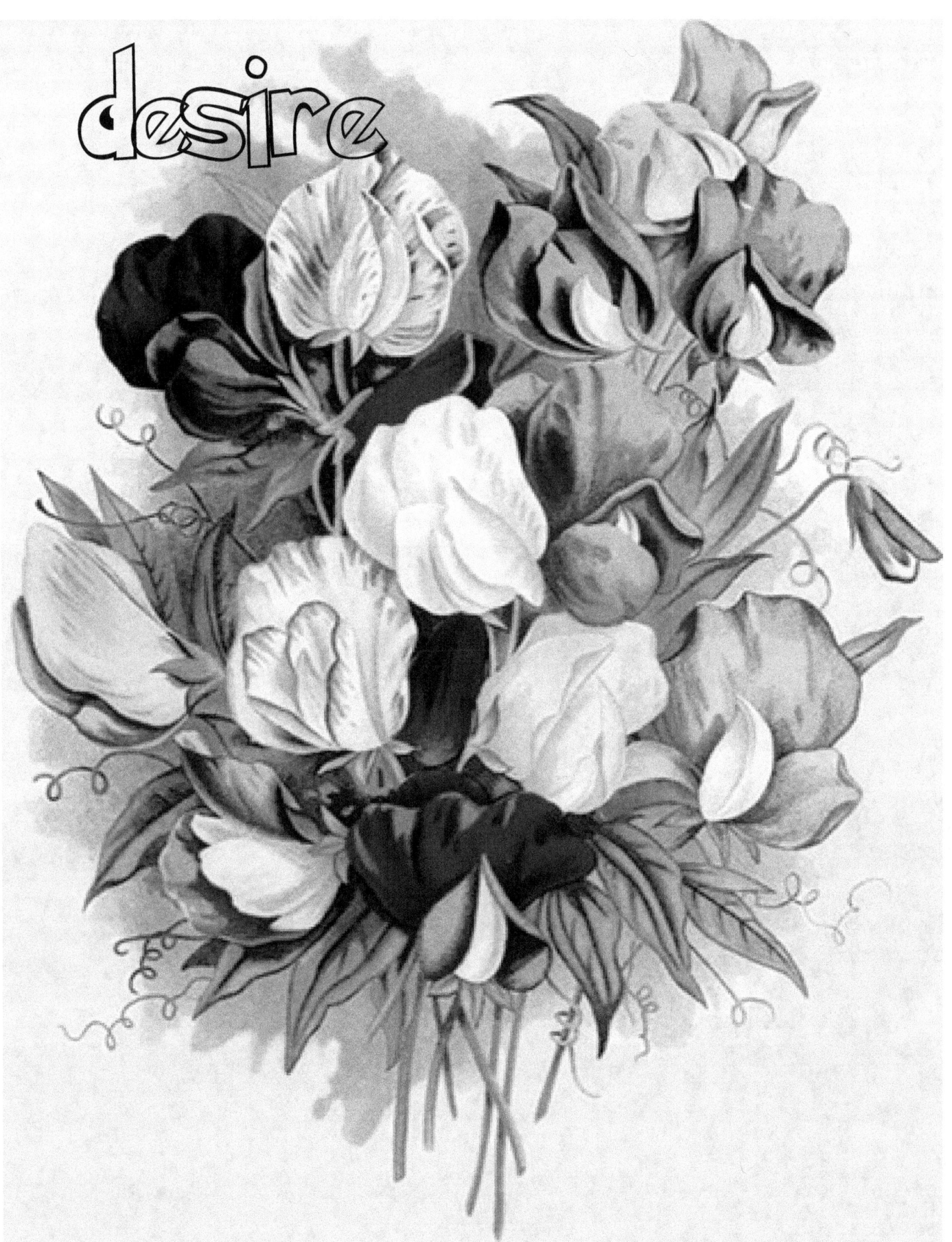

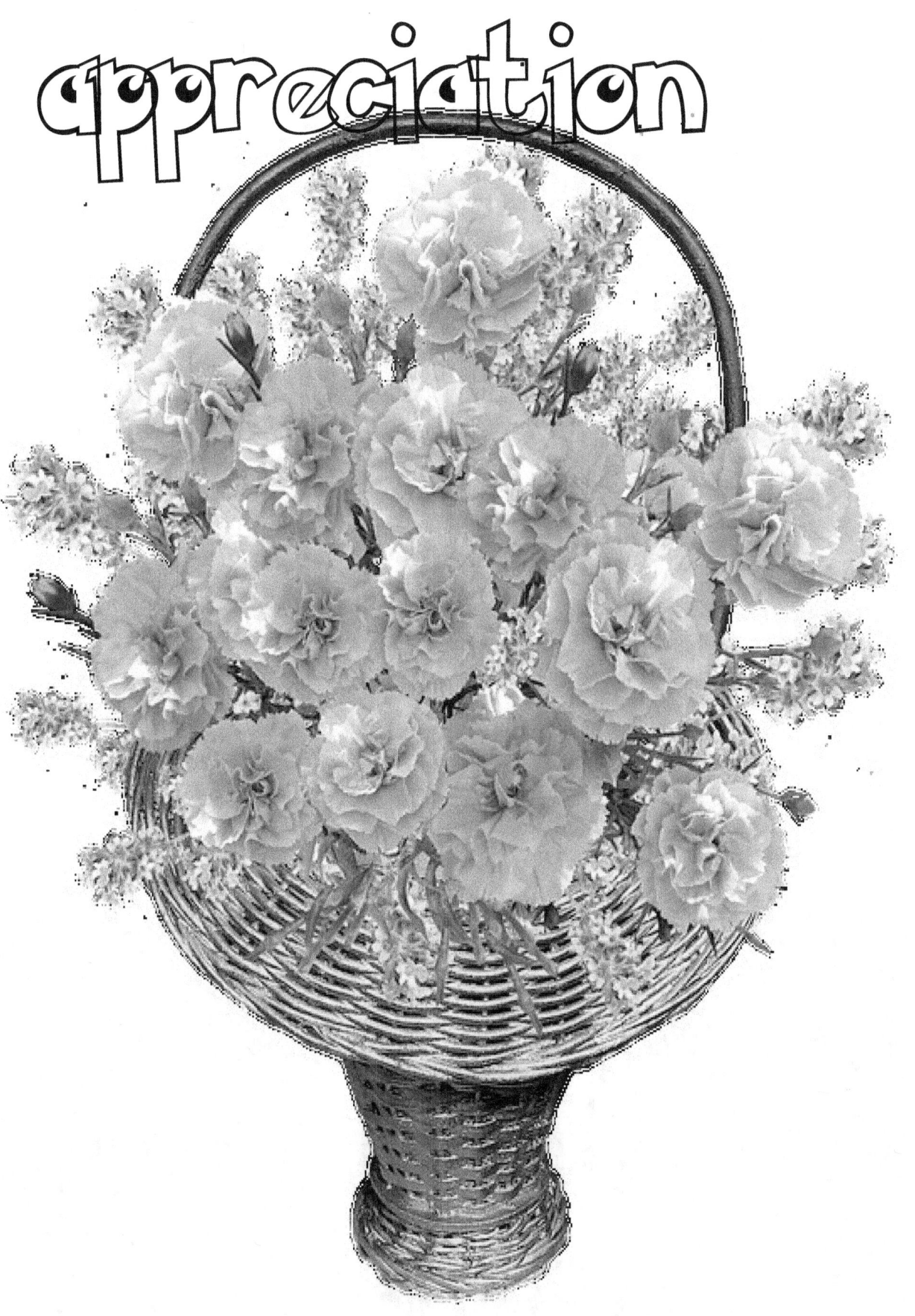

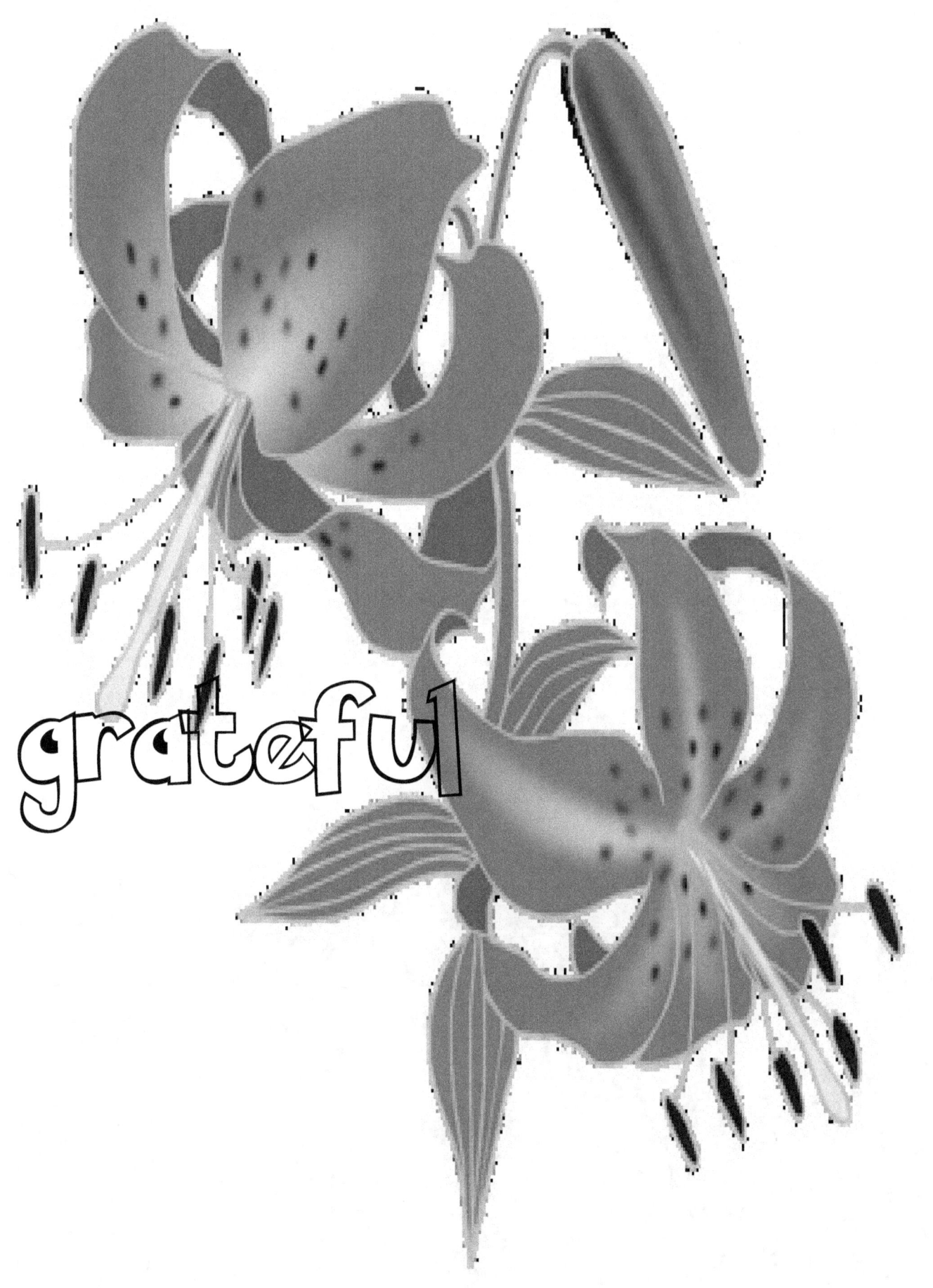

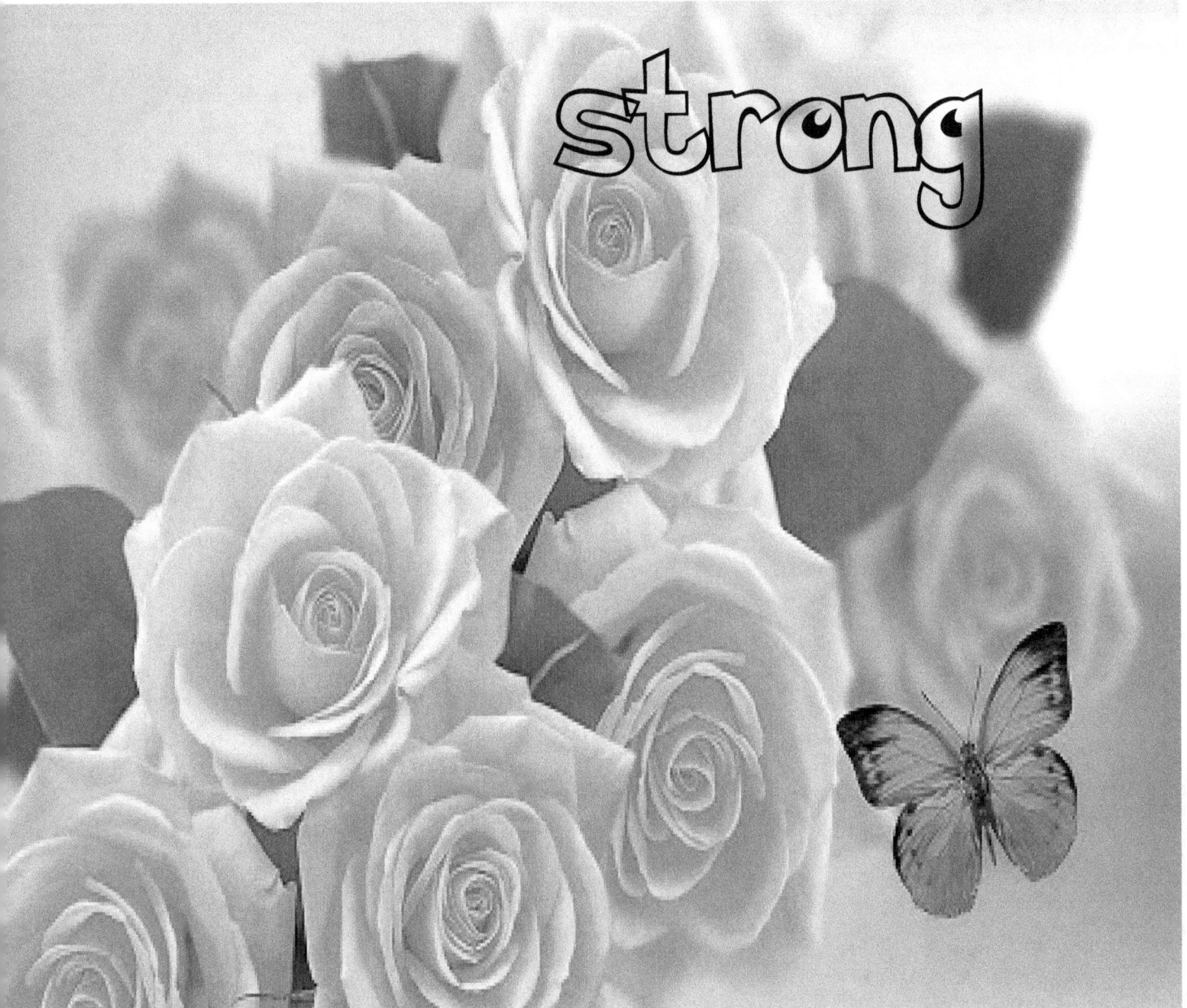

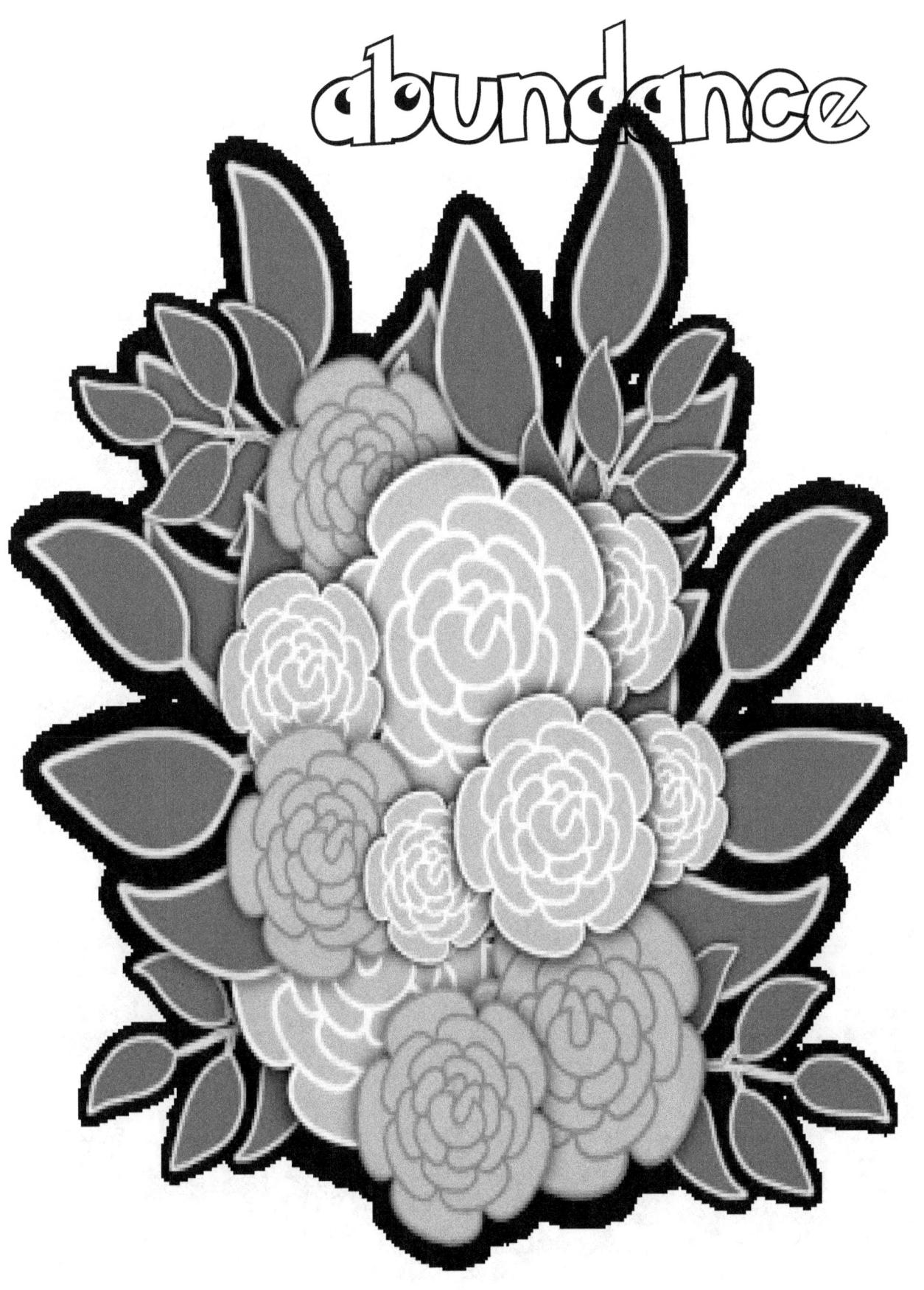

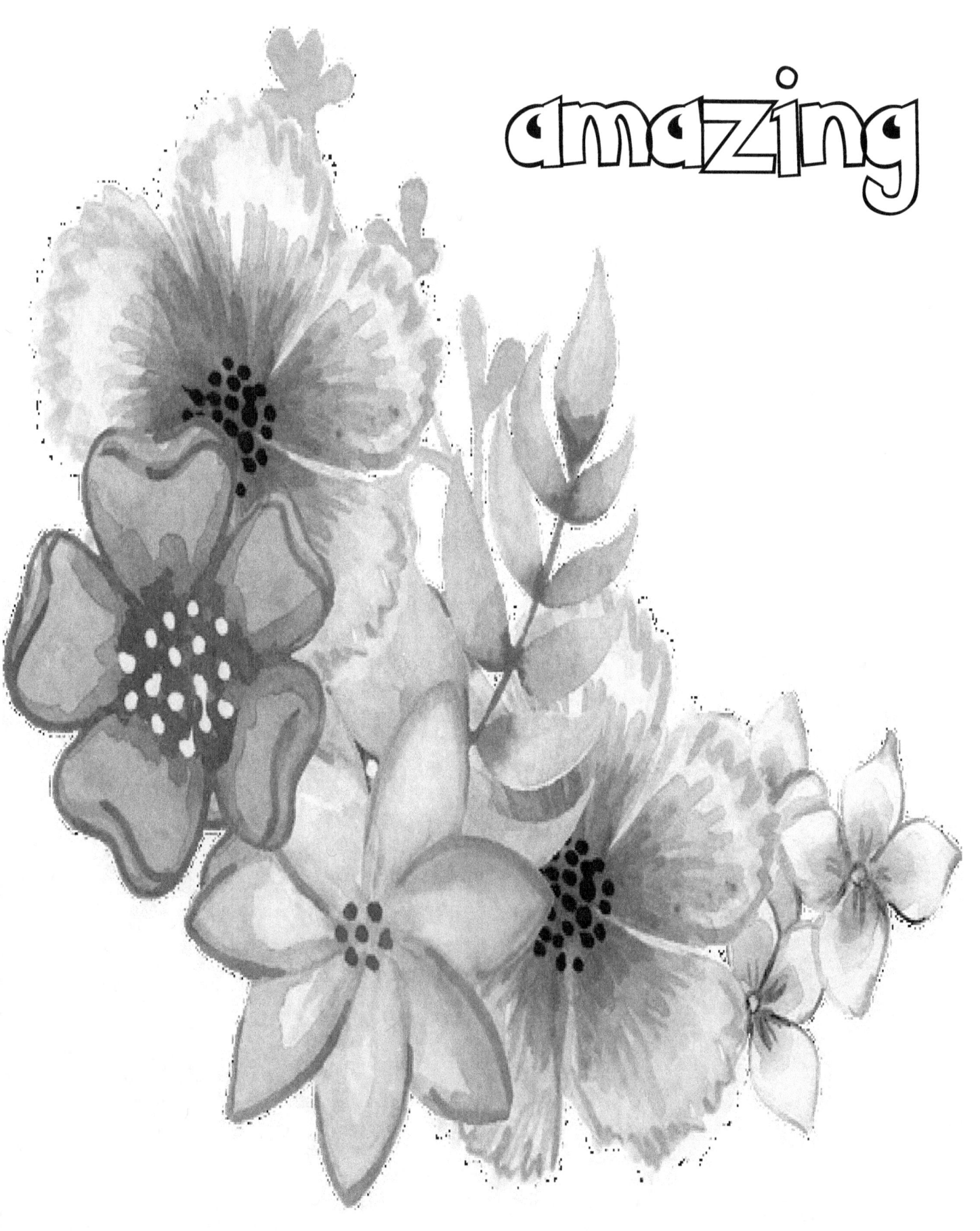

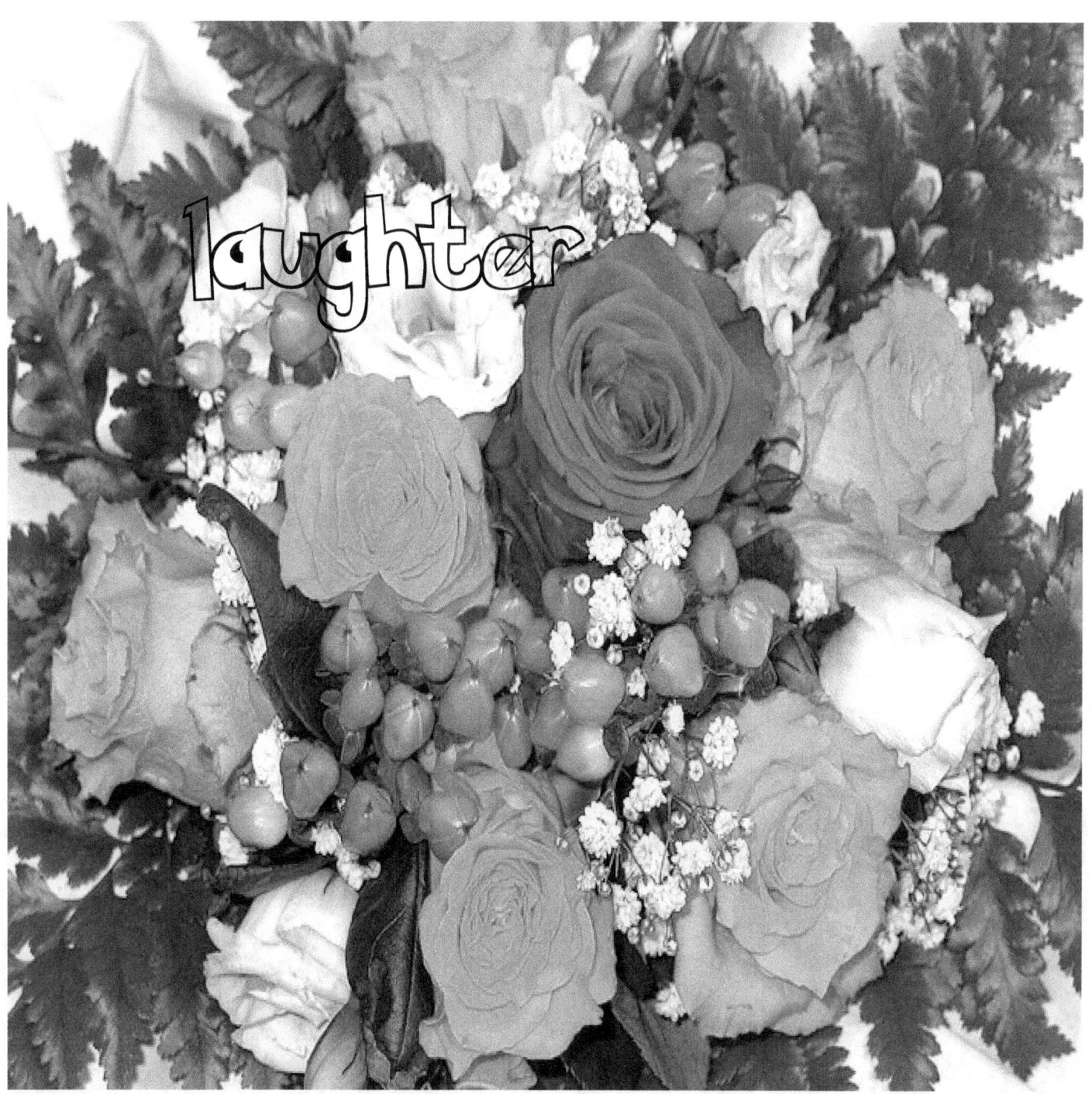

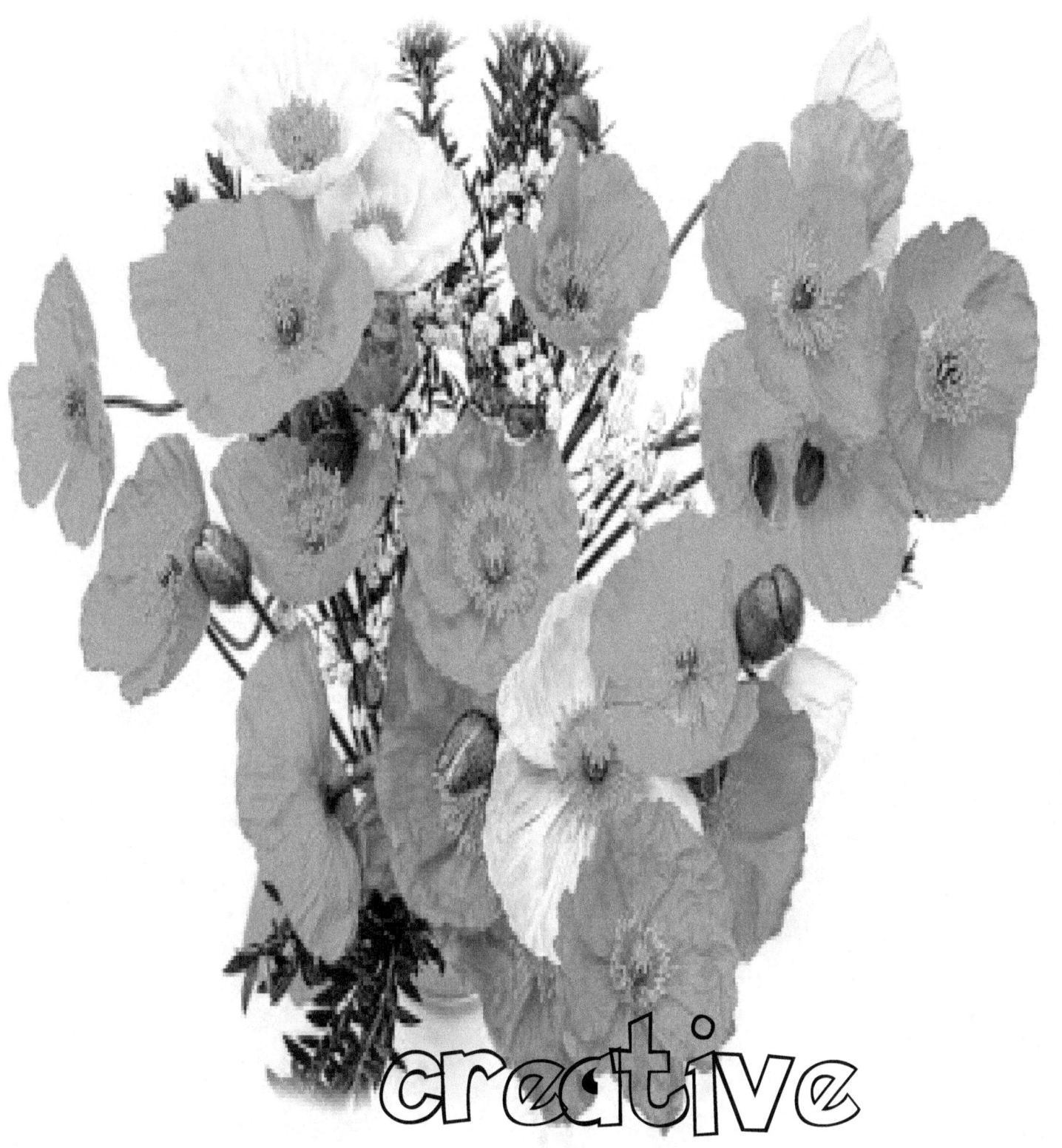

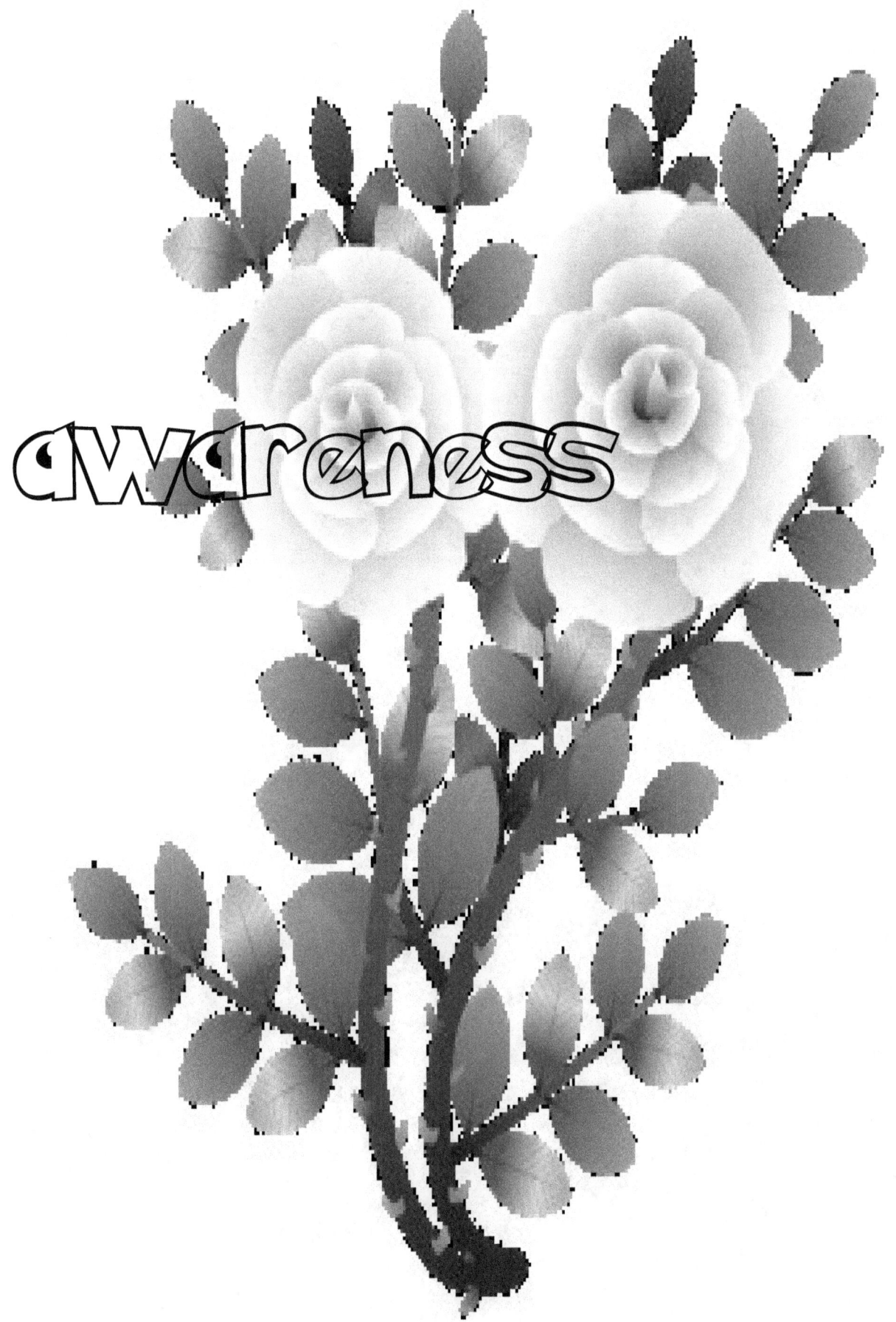

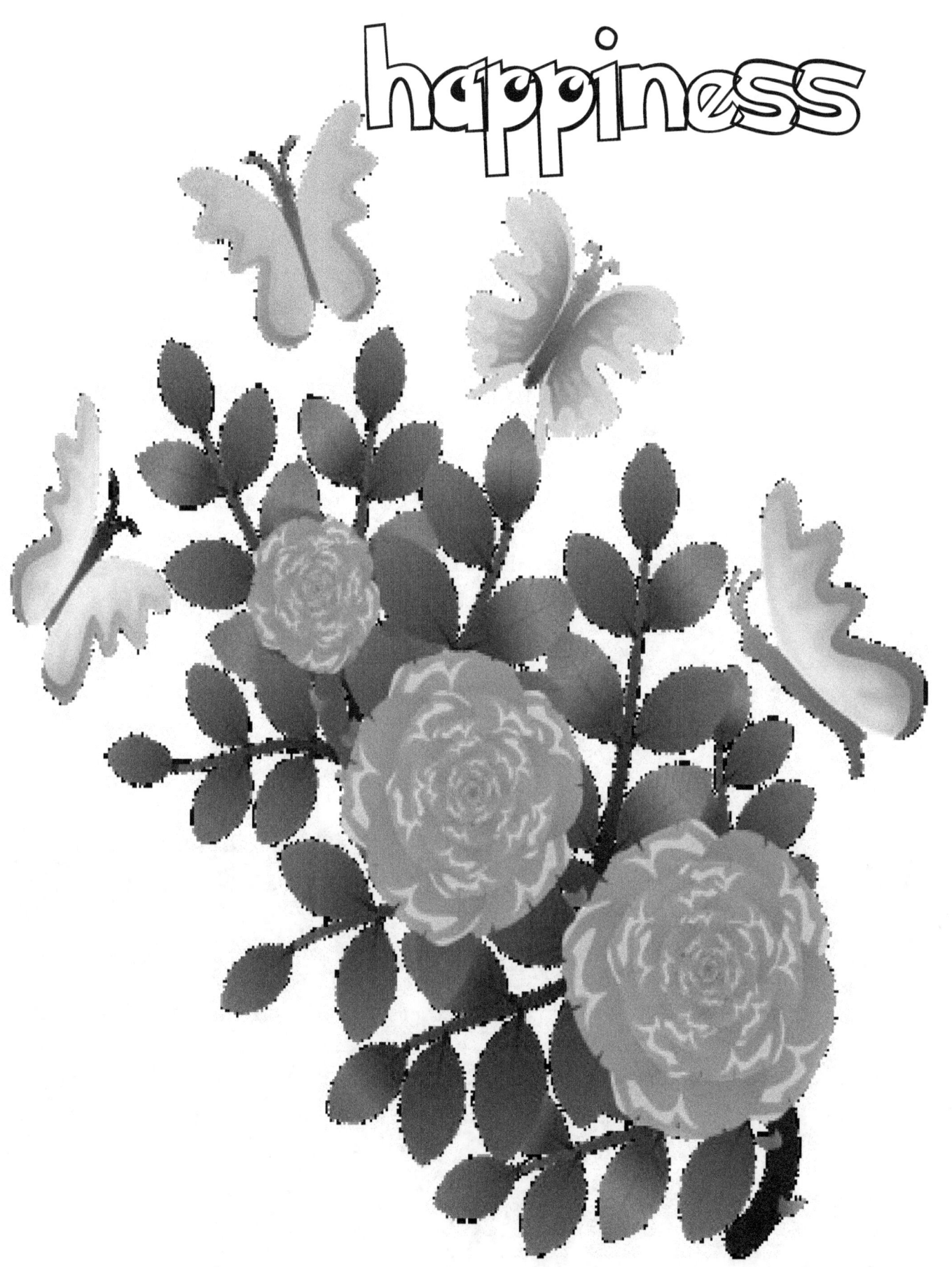

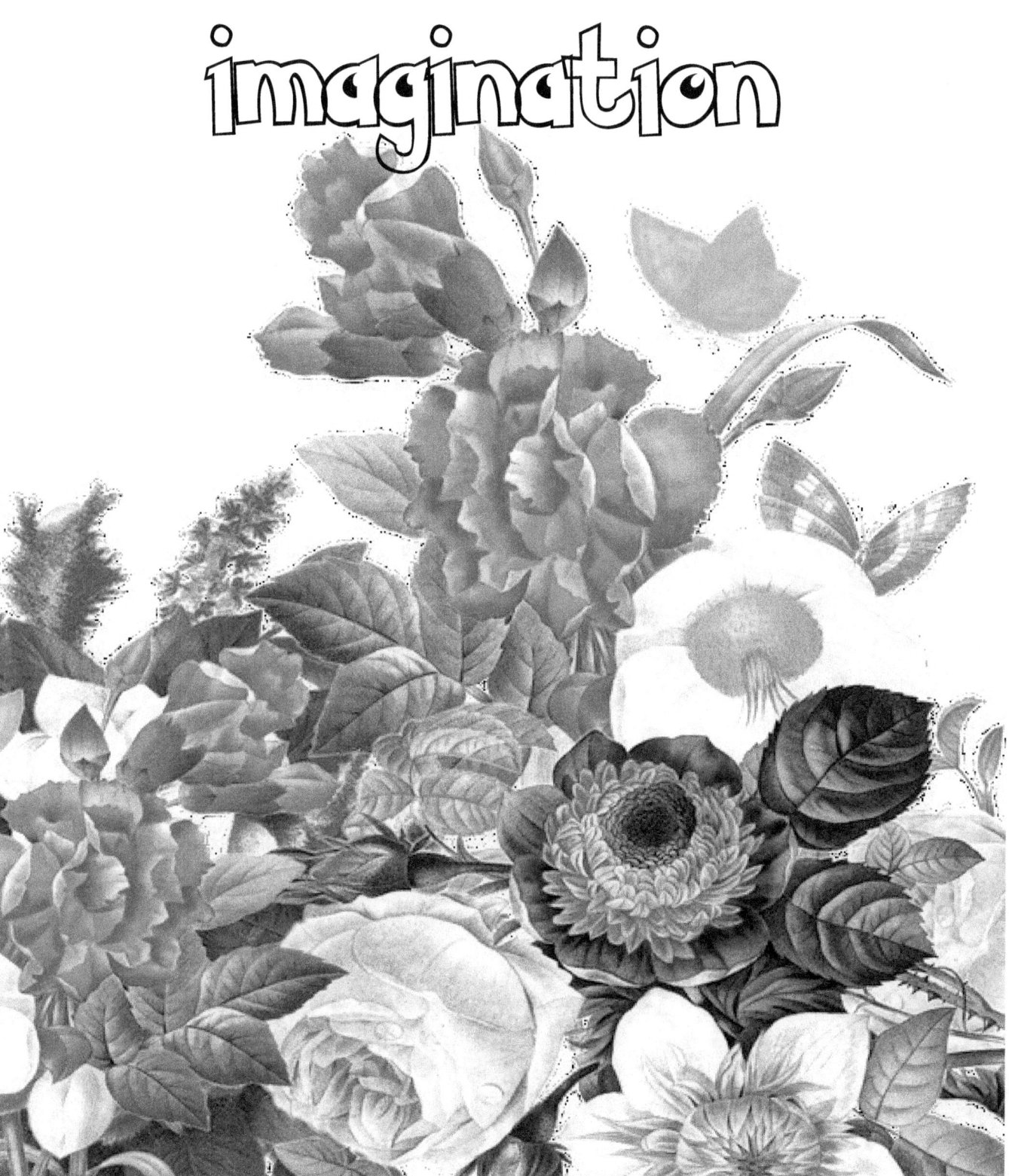

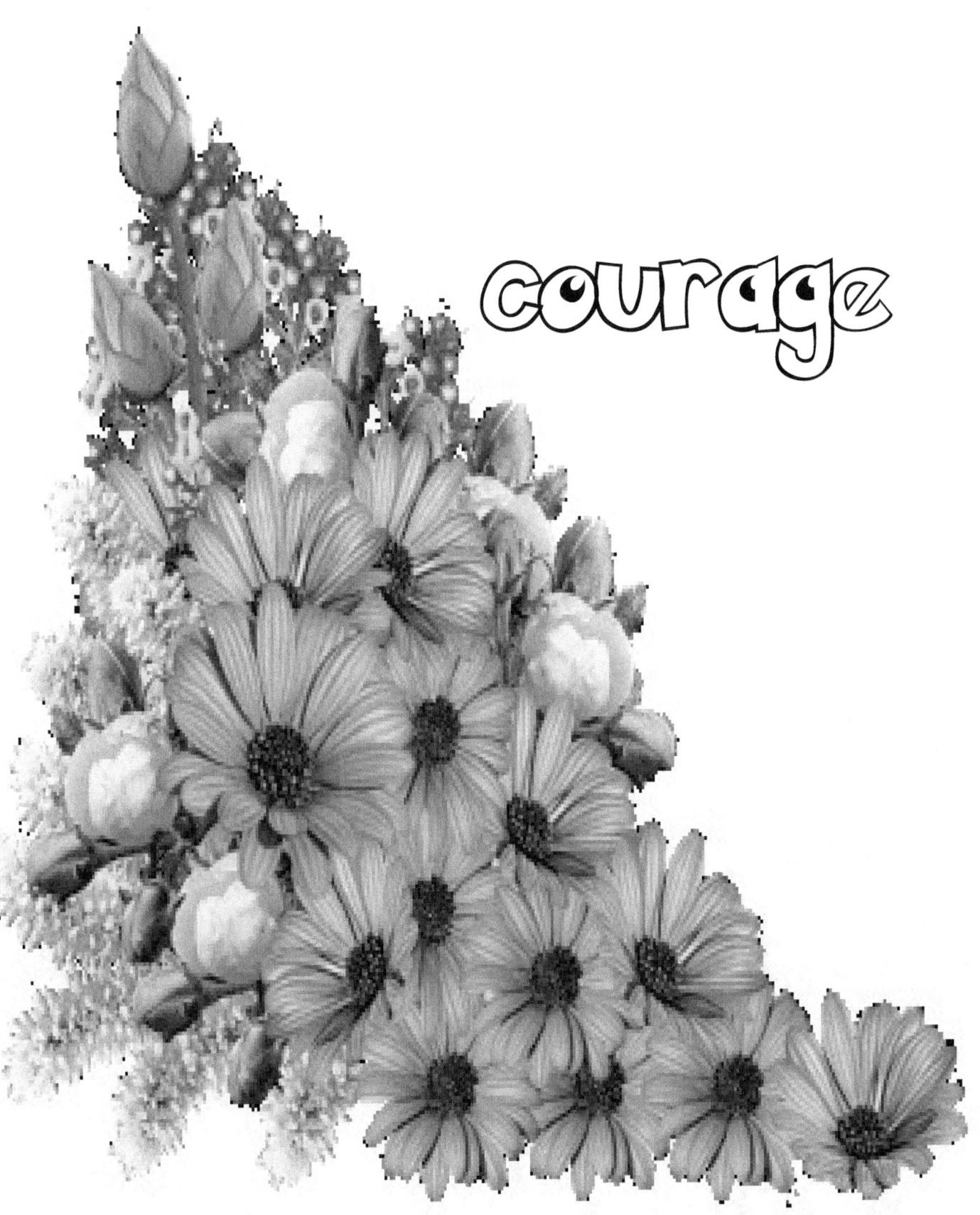

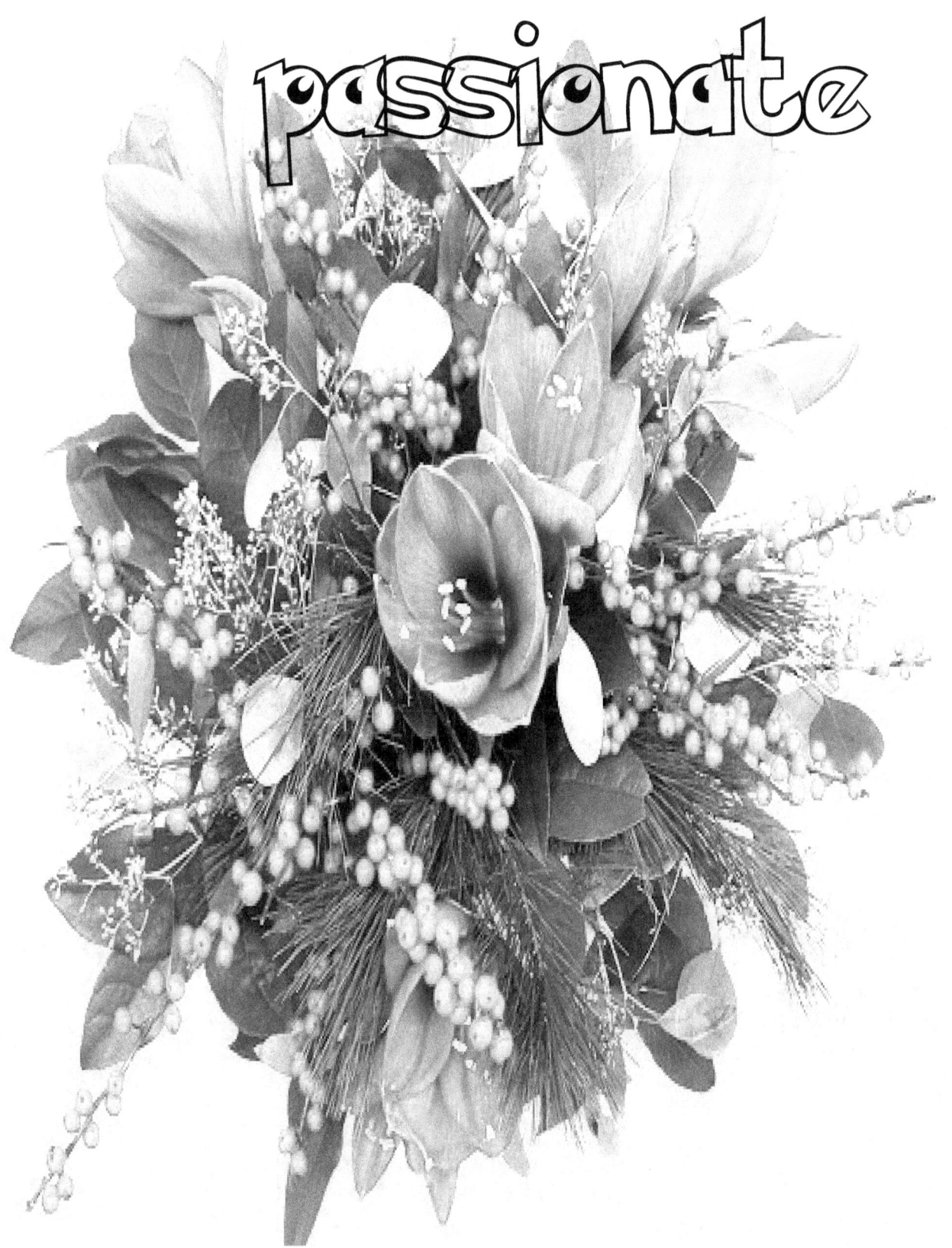

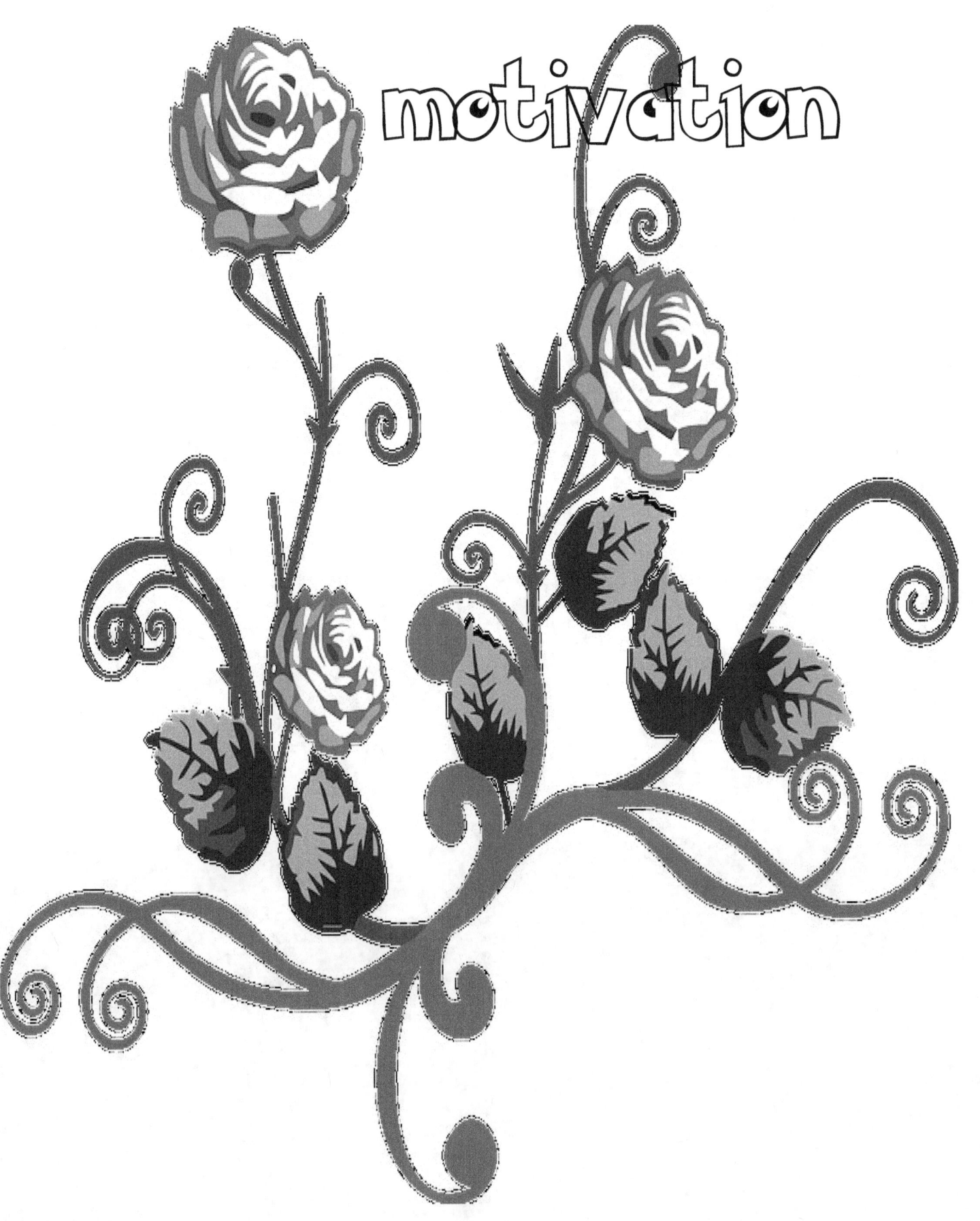

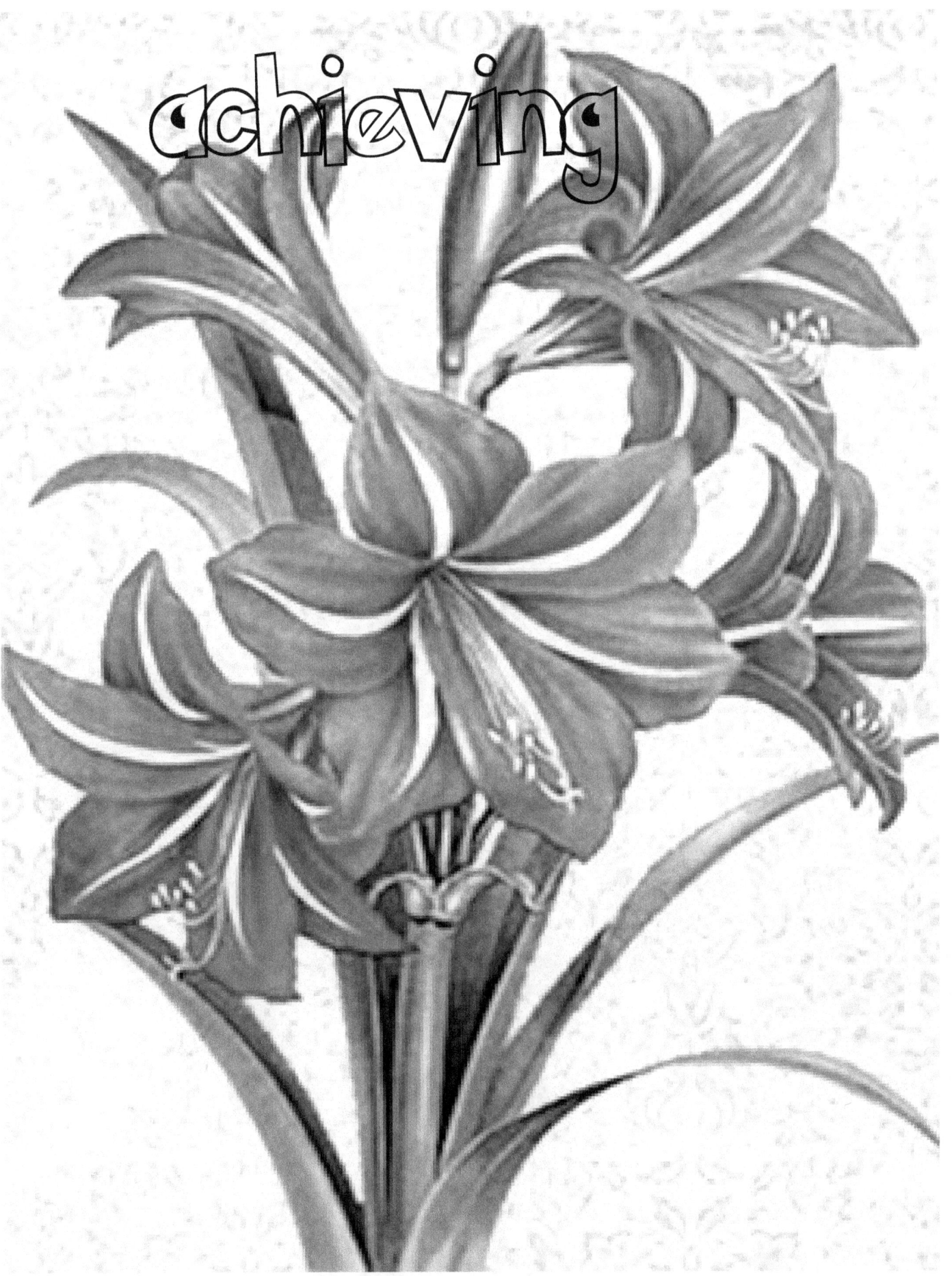

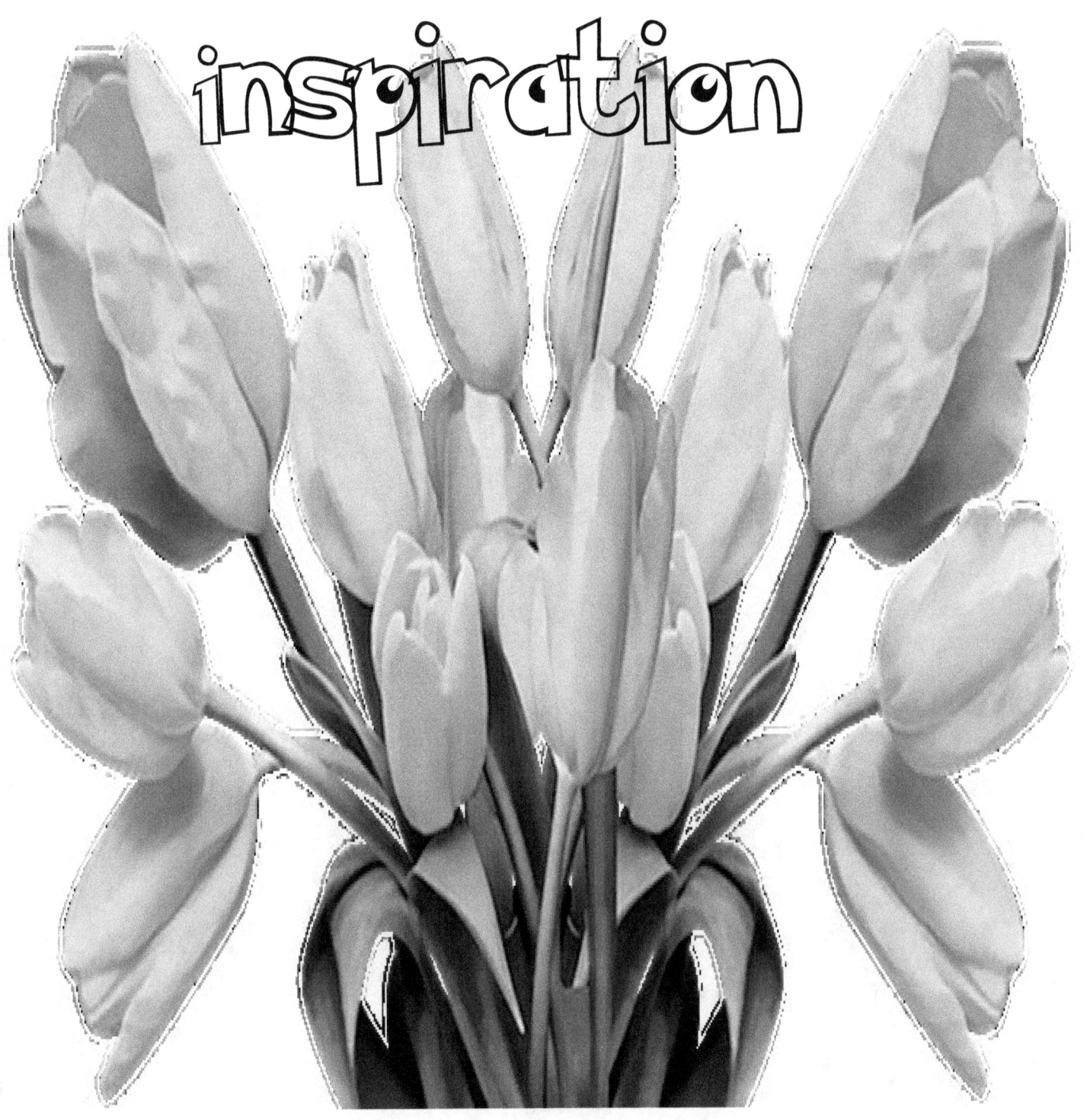

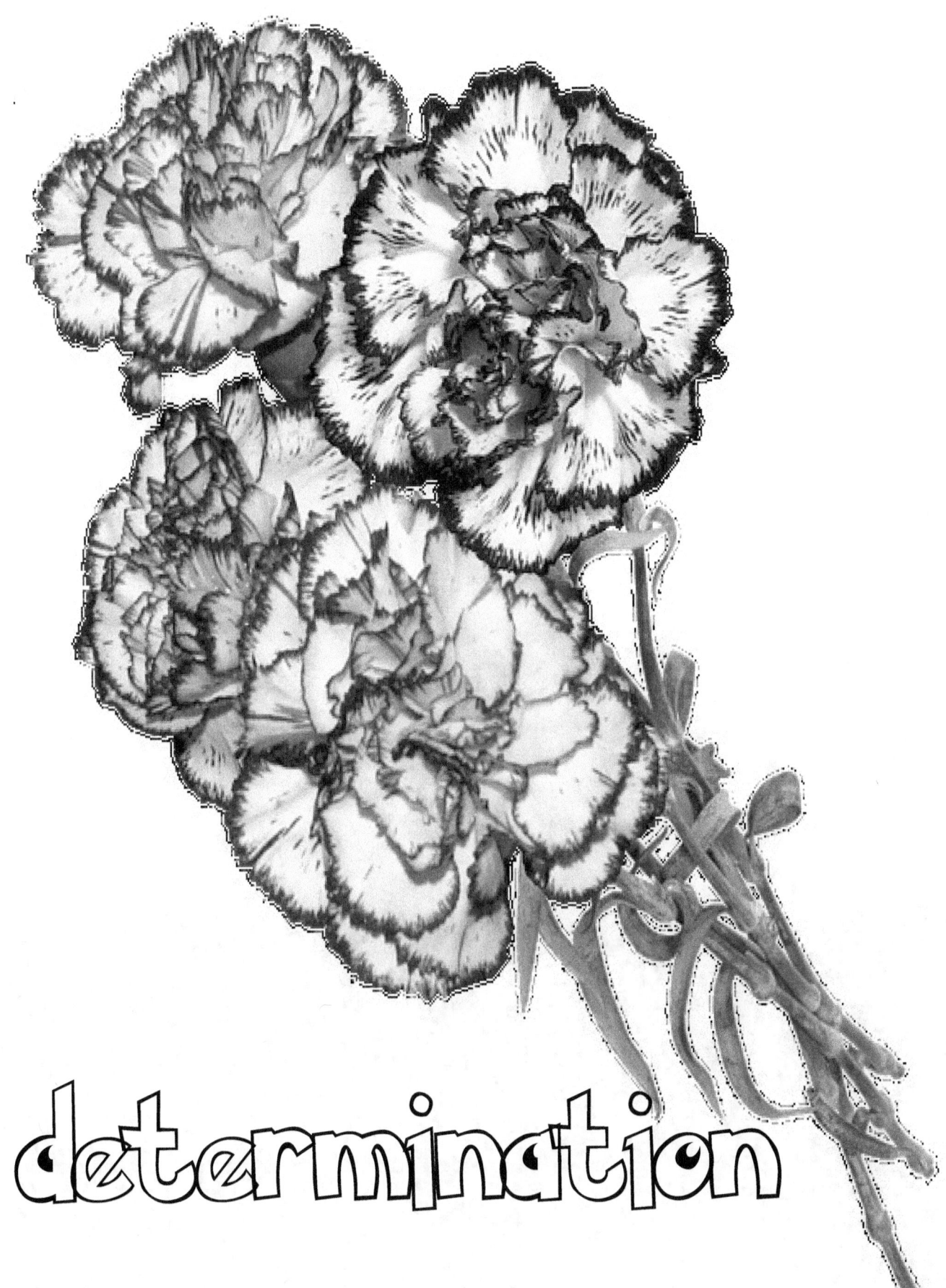

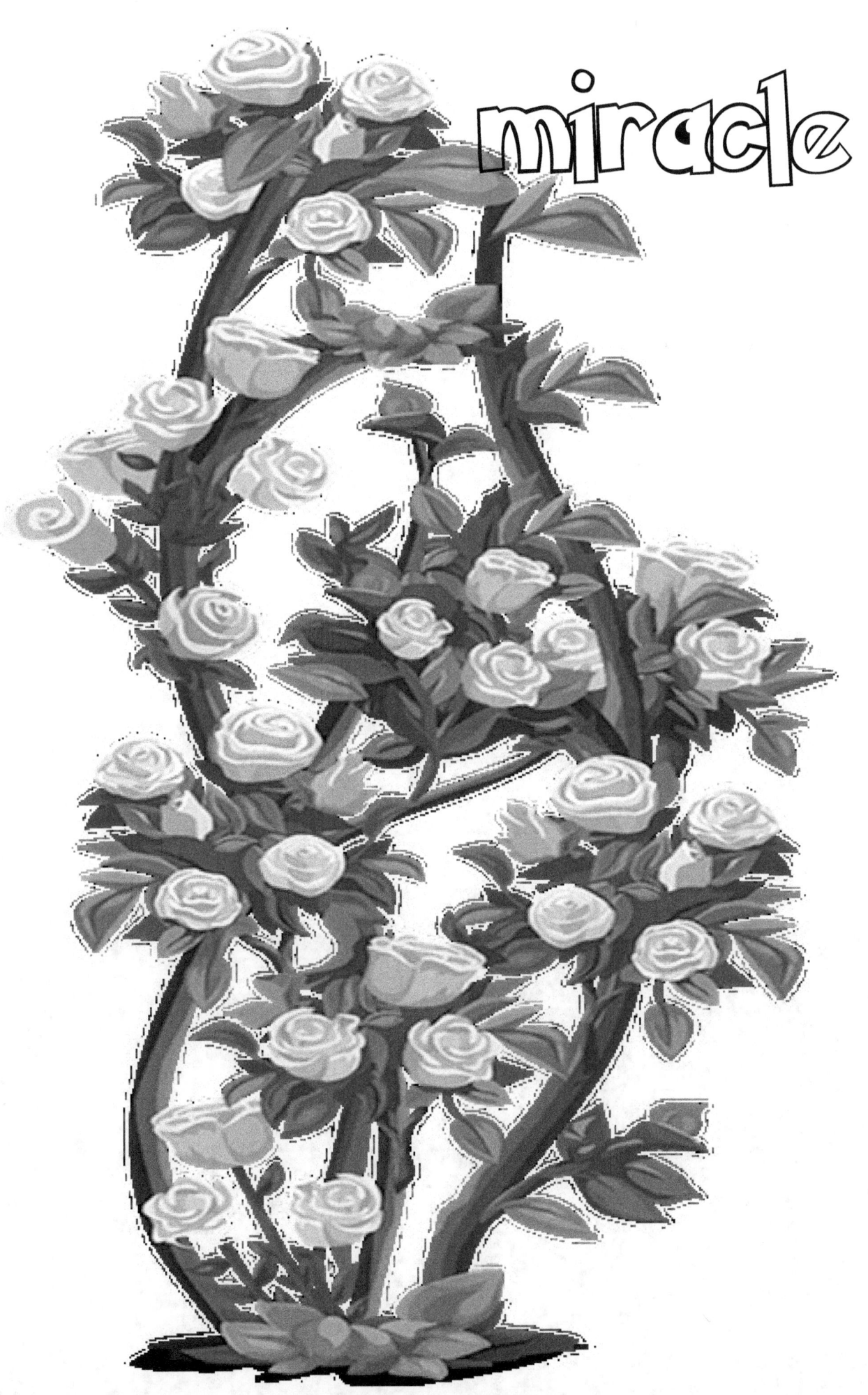

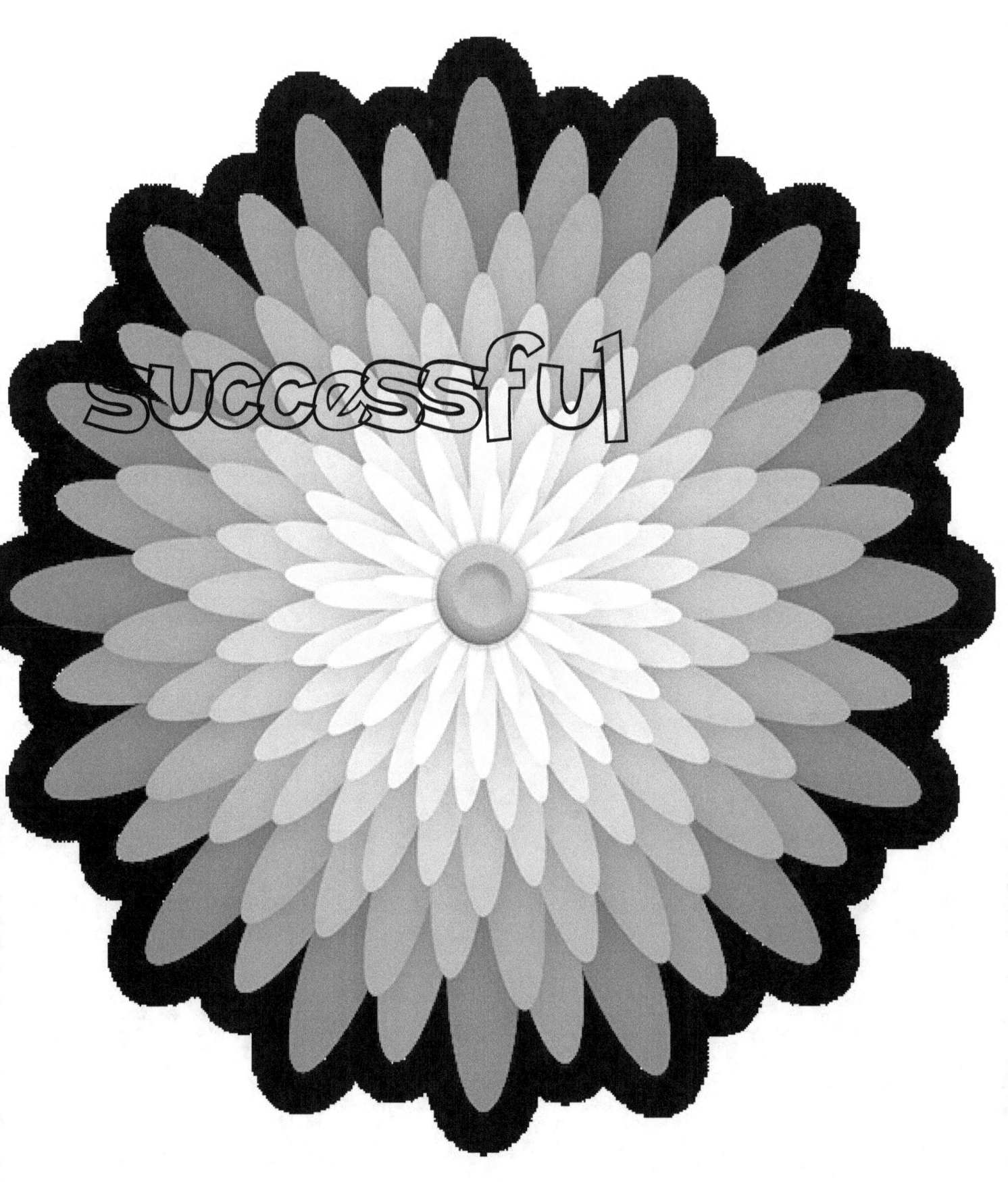

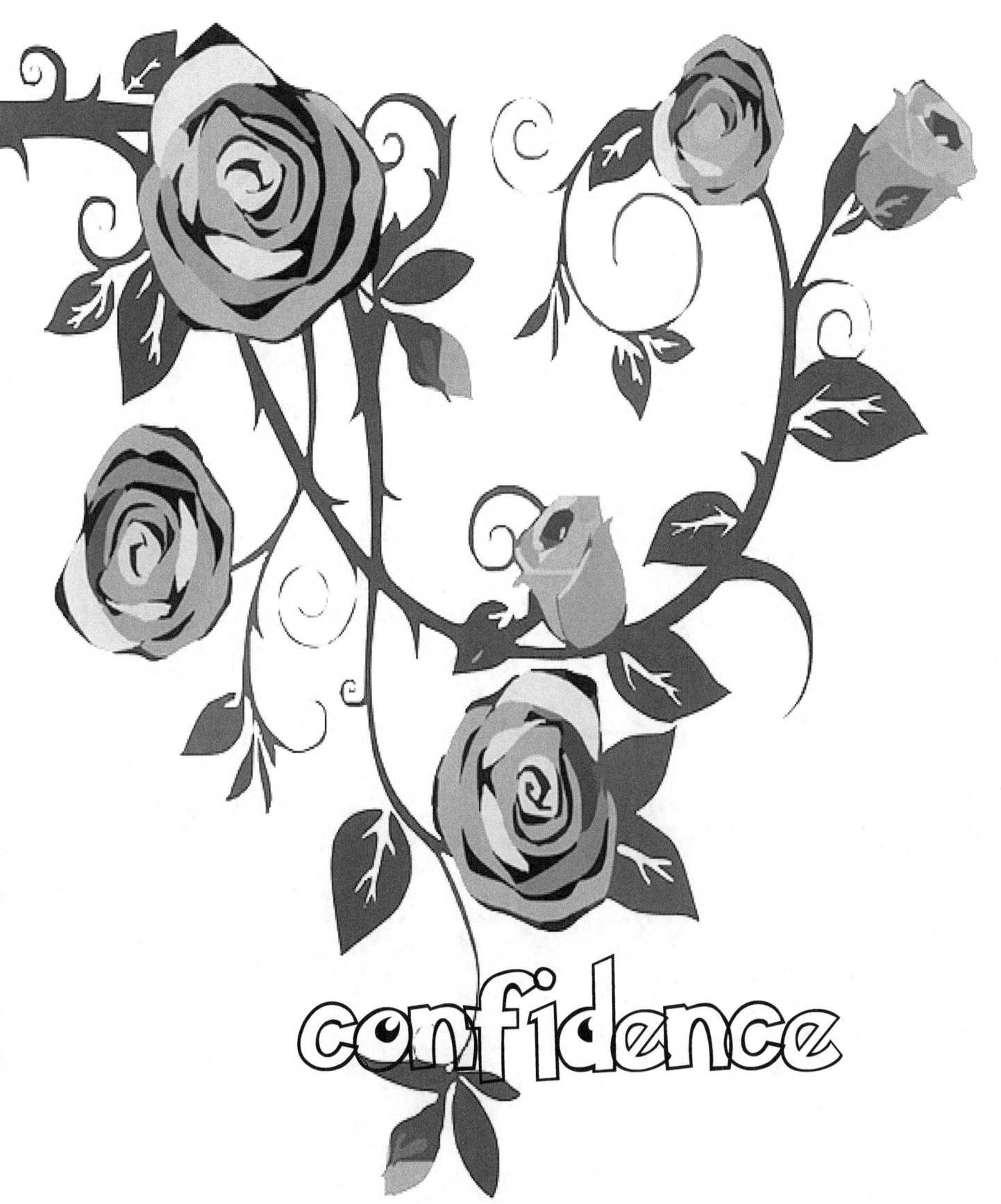

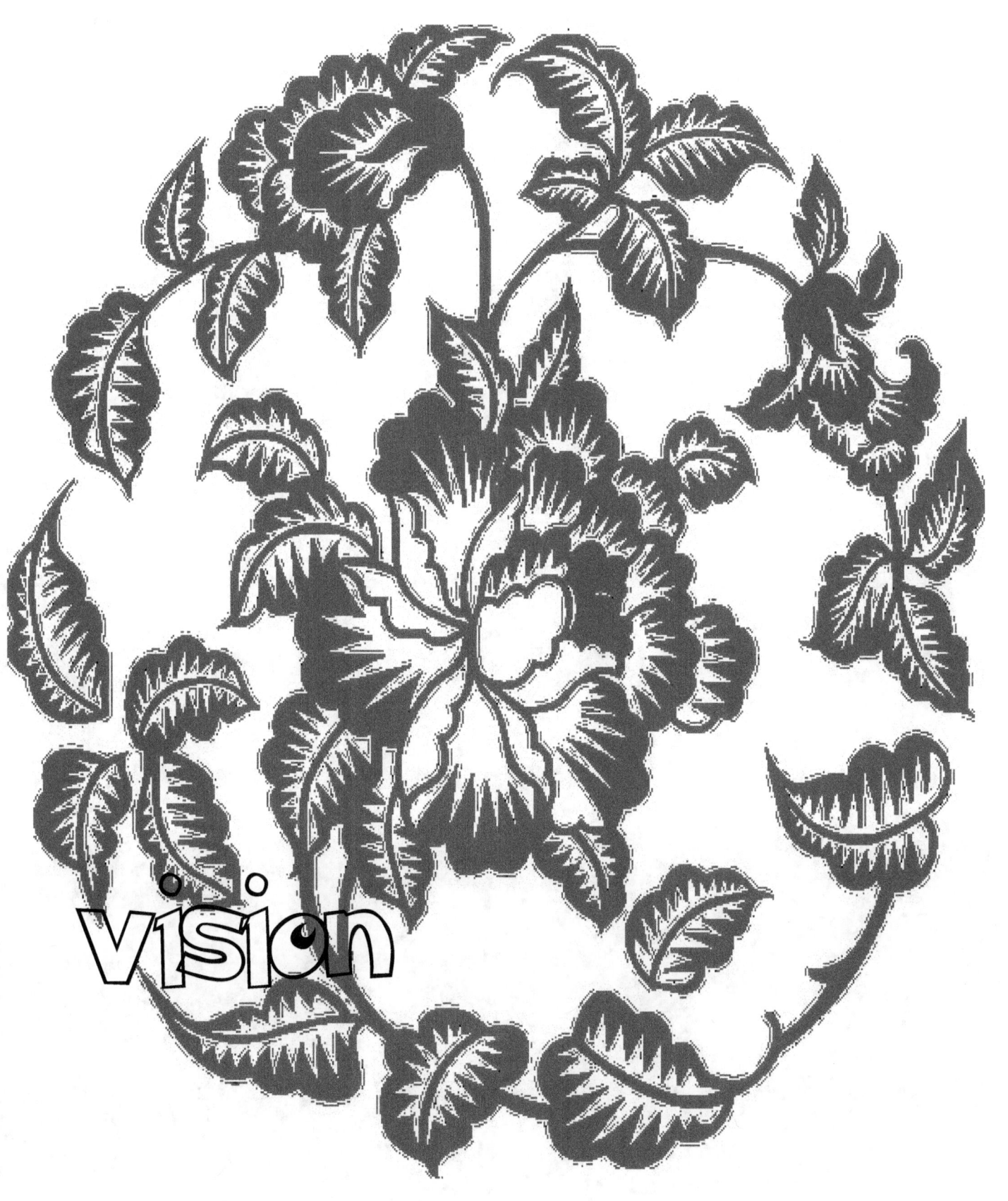

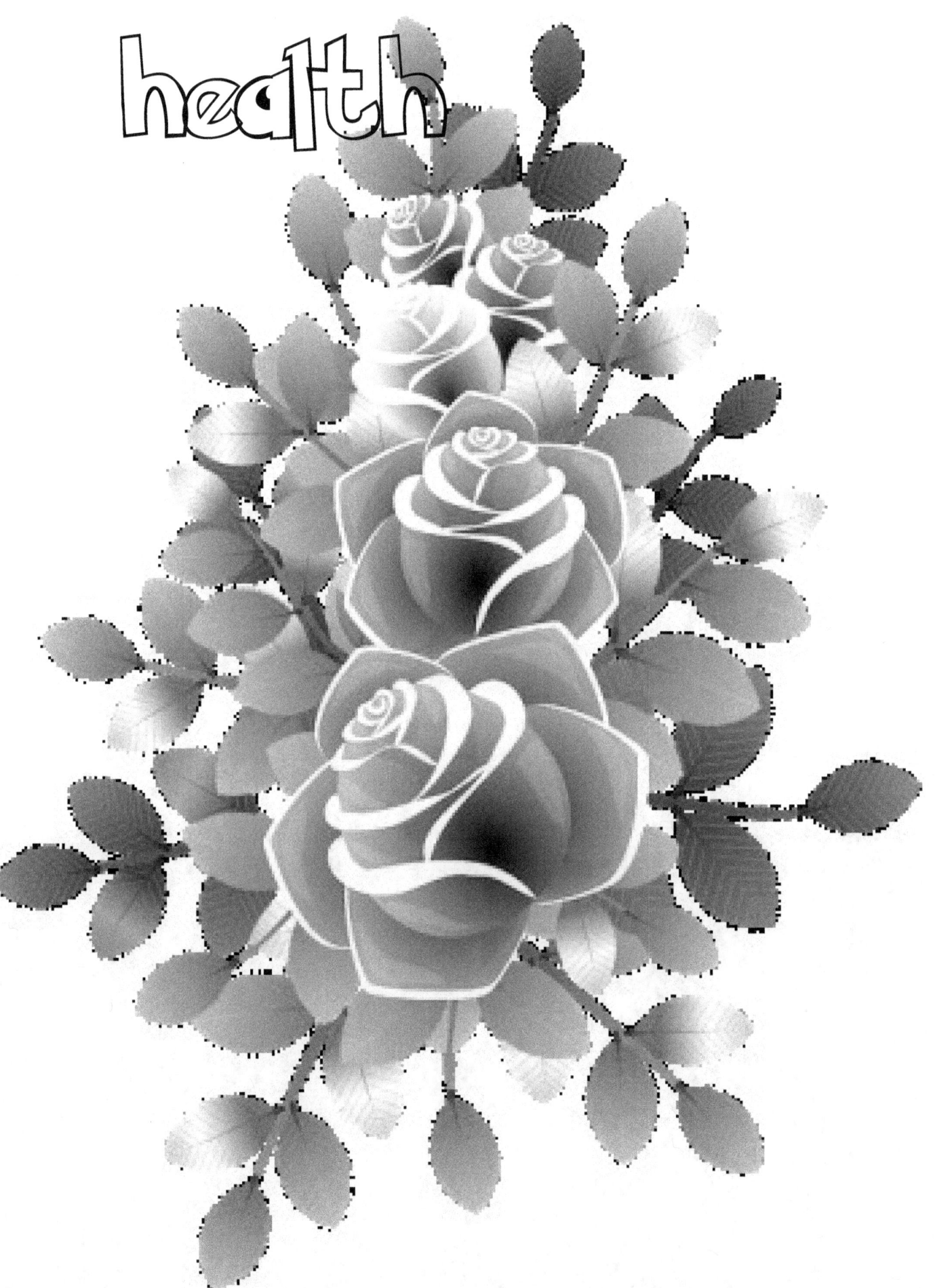

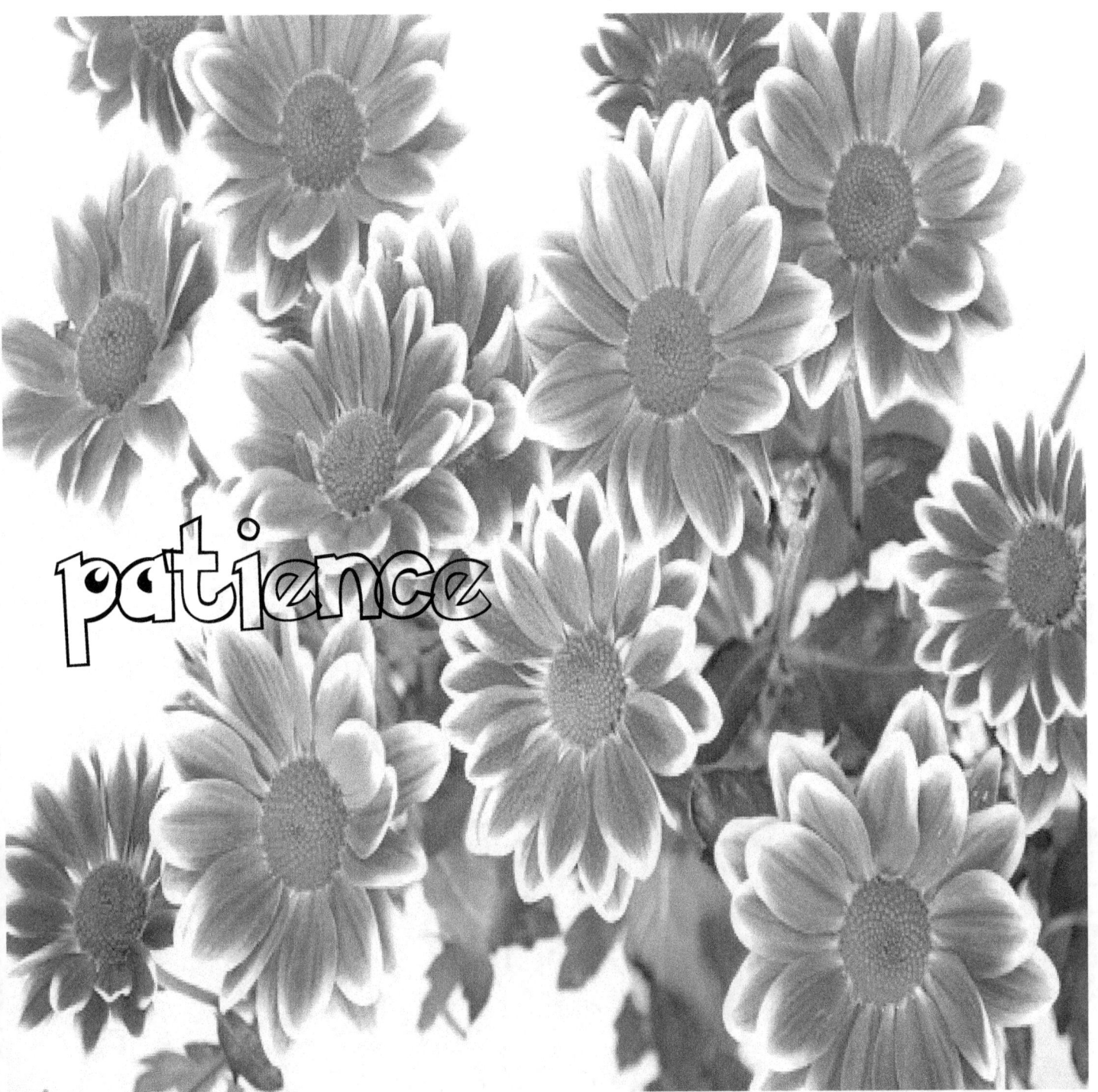

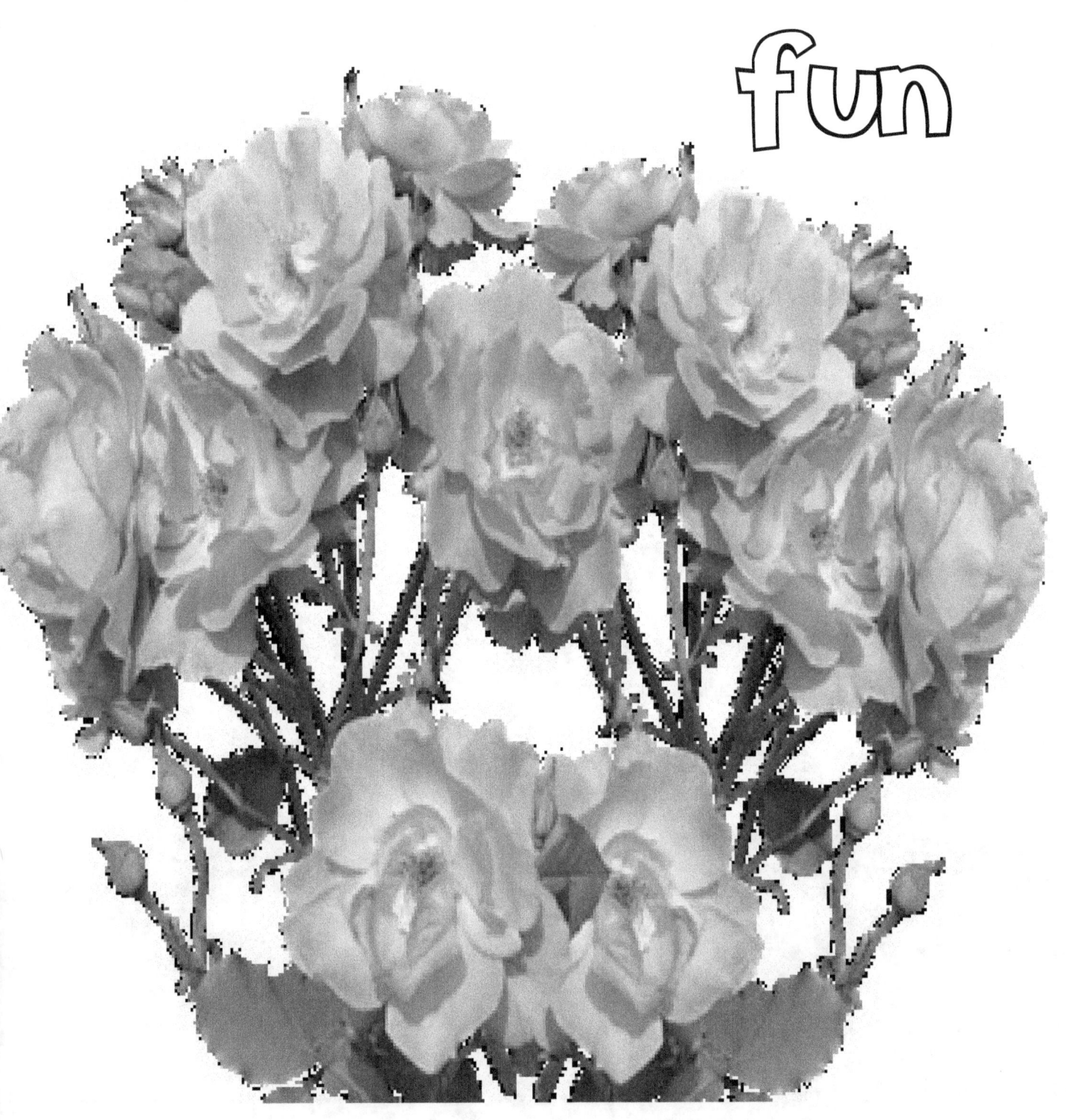

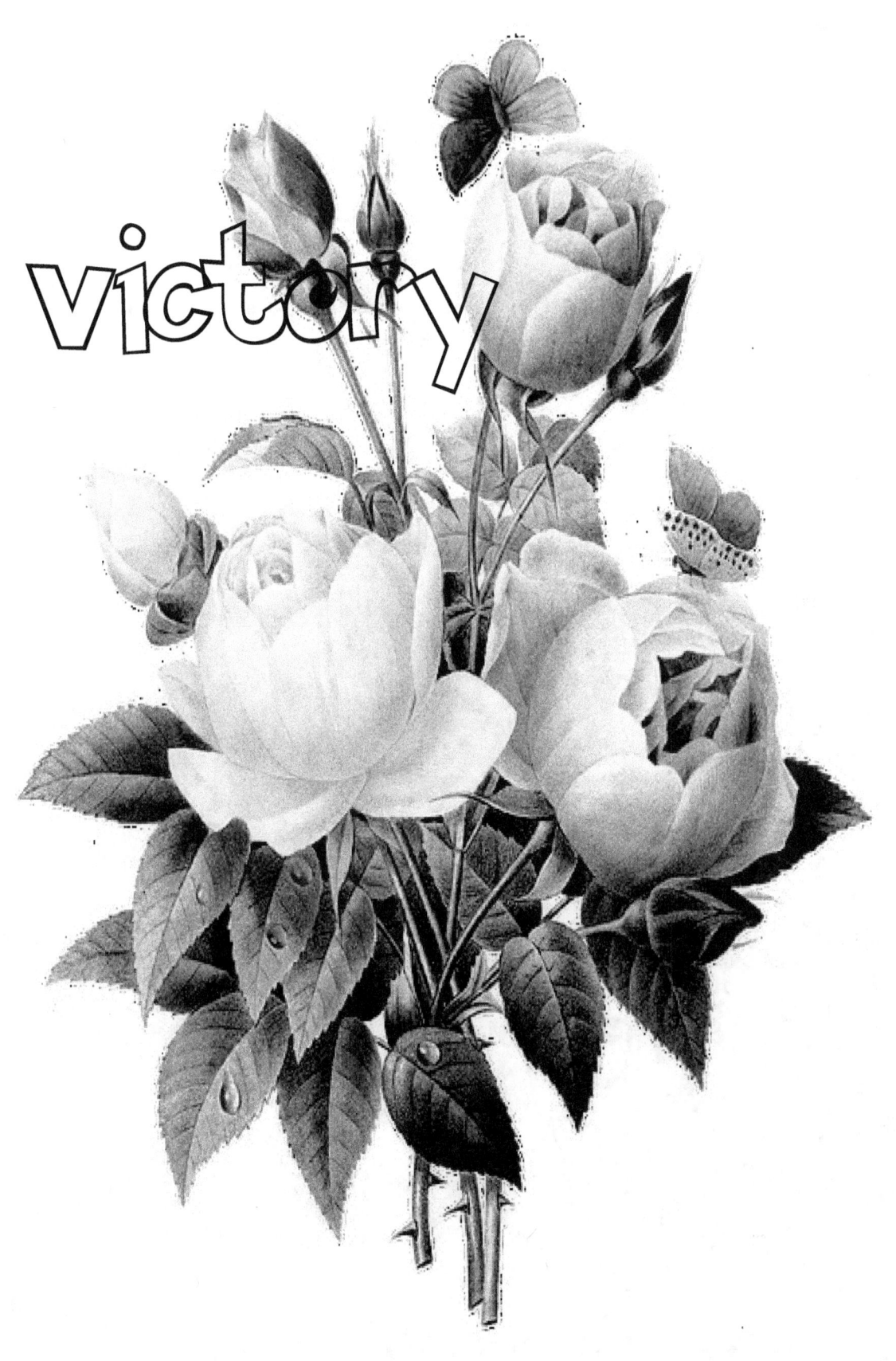

Please leave a review

This coloring book will make wonderful gifts for the whole family and friends.

www.ingramcontent.com/pod-product-compliance
Lightning Source LLC
Chambersburg PA
CBHW062224220526

45471CB00009B/3331